DEREK
ACORAH
HAUNTED

DEREK ACORAH

HAUNTED

Scariest Stories from the UK's no. 1 Psychic

HarperElement
An Imprint of HarperCollins*Publishers*
1 London Bridge Street,
London SE1 9GF

The website address is: www.thorsonselement.com

and *HarperElement* are trademarks of
HarperCollins*Publishers* Ltd

This edition published by HarperCollins*Publishers* 2008

A catalogue record of this book is
available from the British Library

ISBN-13 978-0-00-726741-5
ISBN-10 0-00-726741-X

*Dedicated to the memory of all those whom
we have loved who are no longer with us.
We will meet again.*

Contents

Acknowledgements

I would first like to mention my mother Lily, who passed on to the spirit world in March 2007. She is sorely missed by me and the rest of the family. My mother was my inspiration and, apart from my beloved wife Gwen, was the most important person in my life. I would like to thank all the people who helped me through the period of her passing and to acknowledge the kindness displayed by my close friends and the larger circle of friends who come to see me at theatres up and down the country. Without your compassion and understanding, I would have found that time even harder to bear.

Once again I would like to register my indebtedness to Lizzie Hutchins and all at HarperElement. Both

Gwen and I very much appreciate your unrelenting support.

I cannot forget Paul Flexton and all the staff at Ruggie Media. Our foray into the Sahara this year during the production of *Paranormal Egypt* is a time I shall never forget. It was a magical experience made possible by the good grace of Dr Zahi Hawass and his staff of the Egyptian Council of Antiquities. I must thank Ramy and Sarah Romany, our 'fixers', without whose assistance we might still be wandering around the desert.

As ever, I cannot forget Ray Rodaway, my 'rock' on the road. Travelling the country as we do is not always easy, but Ray makes what could be a bumpy ride so much smoother.

I have to thank Stuart Hobday, my agent, and my wife, Gwen. Without the never-ending support of these two people I doubt whether I could continue.

A special thanks to Patricia Smith for her beautiful and inspirational poetry and for the support she has given me over the years. Special thanks also to Linda and David for their continued dedication in running the Derek Acorah Fan Club. Neither can I forget Talk Derek Acorah, the message board with a difference.

Acknowledgements

Maya and Moonstone do a wonderful job with the help of all the moderators.

Introduction

My name is Derek Acorah. I am a spirit medium. I am clairvoyant, clairaudient and clairsentient and I use my gifts to connect the physical world in which we live to the world beyond to which we are destined to go. When we pass over to the heavenly state, we will be reunited with the loved ones who have passed away before us, be they friends or family, neighbours or members of the animal kingdom who have been special to us during our earthly lives.

Although I was in my thirties before I commenced working for spirit professionally, I realized I had psychic gifts when I was a small boy. I was a mere six years of age when I had my first experience of spirit when I saw my grandfather on the stairway of my grandmother's home. He had passed over to the world of spirit some years prior to my birth.

Over the years I worked first as a medium conducting sittings for people on a one-to-one basis and then progressed to taking part in radio programmes in the days when media mediumship was in its infancy. I went on to appear on television programmes, principally *The Psychic Zone*, *Livetime*, *Psychic Livetime* and *Derek Acorah's Predictions* with Granada Breeze, the satellite arm of Granada Television based in Manchester.

Just before Granada Breeze ceased to broadcast, I agreed to take part in a pilot programme provisionally named 'Haunting Truths'. That programme went on to become known worldwide as *Most Haunted* and is owned and aired by LivingTV. After appearing in almost 100 programmes and numerous *Most Haunted Live* broadcasts, at the end of series 5 I decided to move on. I agreed to take part in one last series and three more *Most Haunted Live* programmes and completed my commitment to the programme in October 2005.

By that time I had already commenced filming a new programme for LivingTV. It was known as *Derek Acorah's Ghost Towns*. Working with Danniella Westbrook and Angus Purden on the first two series and with Myleene Klass and Rhodri Owen on the third series, I had a wonderful time travelling up and down the country visiting reputedly haunted locations. Unlike the format of *Most Haunted*, these locations were not well-known historic buildings but homes, shops and other more insignificant places. Nonetheless they were often exceedingly haunted in their own right.

The summer of 2007 brought the realization of an ambition I had had for many years when LivingTV commissioned, through Ruggie Media, a new programme. It was to be named *Paranormal Egypt*. Making eight programmes covering Egypt's incredible history and visiting locations not normally open to the public was a real privilege. The memories will remain with me for the rest of my life.

I am still working hard and have many projects in line for the future. I am continuing with my theatre tours, which encompass the whole of the UK and Ireland, and have plans to work further afield this year.

I have made many new friends and I have also been fortunate in rekindling some old friendships. I am looking forward, as I write this in January 2008, to many more years of working for spirit.

CHAPTER ONE

Channelling

First of all, I would like to say a few words regarding my work as a spirit medium.

For those who do not understand what a medium is, I would like to explain that a person with mediumistic gifts is someone who is able to communicate with people who have passed away – passed over to the spirit world or, as I like to call it, to the higher side of life.

Mediumistic communication with spirit people is achieved through clairvoyance, clairaudience or clairsentience. The word 'clairvoyance' literally means 'clear seeing', i.e. a person who is clairvoyant can see, either subjectively (in their mind's eye) or objectively (with their physical eyes), a spirit person or a symbol passed on to them by people in the spiritual realms. Clairaudience is the gift of 'clear hearing'. This happens when an individual receives verbal communication from people in the spirit world. Clairsentience, or 'clear feeling', is when a person feels energies. These are not necessarily energies from the spirit world; they may be energies from the living too.

All mediums are deeply psychic and clairsentient. Many are both clairsentient and either clairaudient or clairvoyant. Others, such as myself, are gifted in all three areas.

A medium can also often see the auras of people or animals. The aura is the individual energy field that surrounds every living being. It consists of bands of coloured energies denoting the physical health and emotional state of that being, and so a medium who is aware of it can gain information as to how a particular person or animal is feeling, whether there has been illness or emotional upset or, indeed, whether there is the imminent prospect of some ailment.

I feel it is important to point out that although a medium may be very gifted, when they are not working and open to spiritual vibrations, they are only as psychic as everybody else. So they are just as likely as the next person to lose an item, to have an unexpected flat tyre, to forget something or to experience any one of life's ups and downs. It is pointless making that hackneyed quip 'You didn't see that one coming, did you?' when a mishap occurs in a medium's daily life. If any of you have made this observation, no doubt you have received a wry smile from the medium in question. The point is that it is only when a medium has prepared themselves for psychic work and has opened themselves up to the vibrations and influences of the world of spirit that they are in a position to demonstrate their mediumistic gifts.

By 'opened themselves up', I mean that they expand their consciousness – that part of the brain that houses our psychic side. (We all have it – we are all psychic to some degree.) They then become more keenly aware of the atmosphere around them, whether visiting a haunted location or giving a reading to an individual who has requested an insight into their life or an answer to a personal question.

The preparation for such work involves offering up a prayer for self-protection. This request for protection is of paramount importance. When I pray to my guides and doorkeepers, I do so for both myself and any other person or persons present with me. I must stress, however, that it is important for each individual to ask for their own protection from negative spirits. If you knowingly enter an alleged haunted location, you cannot leave the responsibility for your protection to the medium alone. You have a duty to yourself.

As well as asking for protection, I would also stress that it is absolutely necessary for mediums to practise the discipline of closing themselves down to spiritual influences when they are not working. To leave oneself open is foolhardy indeed. Not only will the medium become exhausted by the constant draining of their energies, but they won't be living a true and proper life on the physical plane and will therefore lose that important grip on reality that day-to-day life gives.

When I am working on a paranormal investigation, all my psychic and mediumistic senses come into play. I will watch for the slightest movement denoting spiritual activity. I will listen to make sure that I pick up any words spoken by a spirit being. My psychic senses are honed to the energies in a location so that I can glean any recordings contained in the fabric of a building, in the brickwork and wood or even in the ground upon which it stands. I am fully alert and concentrating on the job in hand.

If it happens that a spirit entity appears, I evaluate the emotional state and temperament of that being. I will communicate vocally with it and hope that I will be allowed to hear any responses clairaudiently. If a spirit being does not wish to communicate I then rely upon the help of my spirit guide, Sam, who will act as a go-between conveying messages from the spirit person to me.

At times I come across spirit beings who are behaving in an anti-social manner or causing concern to the current inhabitants of the building in some way. It is on these occasions that I sometimes choose to channel the spirit in an attempt to discover just why they are acting in this way. In order to do this I have to invite the spirit being to enter my aura, i.e. come very close to me and almost overshadow me. This means that the space in which I am standing is now almost occupied by the spirit person as well and I have absorbed that being into my own aura. It is then and only then that the personality of the being I am channelling will be demonstrated through my own physical body. If the spirit was a violent being in their physical life, then I will demonstrate violence. If they were erratic in behaviour, then I will become erratic for the brief time that I am channelling them. In other words, I will become the person that the spirit being was when they were living here on Earth.

What I have found over the past two or three years is that my channelling has been described as me being 'possessed'. This description was used, for example, by certain members of a production company, through their ignorance of the subject, during the making of *Most Haunted*. It didn't matter how many times I requested that these people did not use that description of that aspect of my work, they still did. I suppose that was because it sounded more exciting and 'paranormal' to talk of possession. But I must stress that I have never been possessed.

I have also heard that sometimes people have commented that I might be schizophrenic or psychotic. I am neither. I am a medium. I find it distasteful in the extreme that certain individuals demonstrate their ignorance of mental health conditions or, even worse, refuse to appreciate just how much heartache and trauma the families of people suffering from such conditions have to undergo. If I behaved in such a manner I would be thoroughly ashamed of myself.

Channelling

Channelling is something that I choose to do. It is an educated choice and I make it because I know that I am experienced enough to deal with the situation. I also have an exceedingly strong spirit guide, doorkeepers and spirit helpers who will assist me, and I make sure that I have at least one person with me – in most cases my good friend Ray Rodaway – who is experienced in dealing with the situation when I do choose to channel a spirit entity.

I have found that by channelling a spirit entity I am more able to understand the personality of the person as they were both in their physical life and after their passing. It gives me a greater depth than merely communicating using the gifts of clairvoyance or clairaudience.

CHAPTER TWO

My Beloved Mother

Over the Christmas period of 2006 my mother and her sister, my Aunt Eileen, came to stay with Gwen and me at our home in England. On 27 December we all travelled to Spain and stayed there for a week. During that week my mother was not herself at all, but I did not realize quite how ill she was.

Prior to the Christmas period I had felt unsettled. My mother had kept coming into my mind and I had gained the distinct impression that all was not well, but I had pushed the thought away, as it wasn't something I wished to contemplate. Something told me, though, that this would probably be the last Christmas I would spend in her physical presence, even though she appeared to be well and in good spirits at the time.

Most people are under the impression that, as a medium, I am well aware of any events about to take place in my life, but this is just not the case. We mediums receive nothing for ourselves. We are deeply intuitive and get 'feelings' when unhappy or joyous events are about to take place, but we receive no definitive information from our guides and helpers. To acquire such detail would necessitate a visit to another medium.

Despite my unease, my mother, my aunt, Gwen and I enjoyed the two-day Christmas holiday and all appeared to be well on our trip over to Spain. Within a couple of days, however, my mother was really not herself. Unlike her normal practice, she would stay in bed until quite late in the day and wasn't at all keen on going out and about. Usually she would be enthusiastic about eating out in restaurants and taking trips to the shops, but not this time.

Gwen had arranged our flights home for quite late in the day so that Mum could have what was now her usual lie-in. Lunch-time came and when my aunt went to rouse her, she found she couldn't. She called me through to the bedroom. Then, gradually, Mum woke up properly. I was worried about what was going on, but did not want to take her to a Spanish hospital, as I was sure this would distress her. I urgently needed to get her home, where I knew she would be happier.

When we finally arrived back at my mother's house, I called the doctor. He came out to visit her and advised that she should go to hospital immediately. An ambulance was called and Mum was admitted to the hospital. She was suffering from a breathing complaint. She had been a heavy smoker all her life and now, at 80 years of age, she was suffering the consequences. Her poor body was not receiving enough oxygen. In effect she was suffering from carbon monoxide poisoning.

The weeks dragged by and we were at the beginning of March with Mum still in hospital. After many ups and downs – indeed, many moments when we thought she was lost – she seemed to rally. The doctors told us that there would be no recovery, but that she could return to her home to spend her last few days or weeks there. Mum had in fact been most adamant that she wanted to return home to be with her family for some time. She was unaware that she had little time left.

Arrangements for oxygen supplies were made and Mum arrived home. My sisters who had flown over from their homes in America stayed with her to care for her. My brother Colin and his wife flew over from his home in Spain. My brother Wayne, my sister Barbara and I were resident in England anyway. So Mum was happy. She had almost her whole family around her – her sons, her daughters and her beloved sister. The only person missing was Fred, my dad, who had passed over to spirit some seven years earlier.

After only three short weeks, Mum suddenly relapsed and then within a day or two she was gone. She had gone to join Fred and the rest of her family in the world of spirit.

To say I was devastated would be an understatement. Again, although I am a medium, this does not mean that I cannot love people with all my heart and then watch them pass over to the spirit world without missing their physical presence. I, too, miss not being able to pick up the telephone and have a conversation. I miss not being able to call in at my parents' home and share a cup of tea with them whilst chatting about what has been going on in my life. I miss an arm around my shoulders and a soft kiss on the cheek. I miss my loved ones as surely and as sorely as anybody who does not possess mediumistic gifts.

My grief seemed insurmountable. I prayed that Mum would return quite soon and assure me that all was well and that she had met up with my dad once more.

The day of Mum's funeral came and went. It was a warm, sunny day. Mum's wish was fulfilled in that her final journey was made in a coach drawn by black horses. My sisters had arranged for two doves to be released after the service. As the birds flew up towards the sun, I bid a last goodbye to the earthly parental ties. Mum and Dad were free now and together.

A few weeks later I woke early one morning. I got out of bed and went downstairs to be greeted by our dogs, Jack and Penny. Their tails wagging frantically, they approved of the opportunity of an early-morning run around the garden.

After letting them out, I put the kettle on for coffee and, whilst it boiled, watched as the two dogs cavorted and gambolled around the garden. When I had made my coffee, I let them back into the kitchen, where they settled down once more to catch up on their sleep.

As I sat at the kitchen table, I heard Mindy, one of our cats, miaowing from another room. I opened the door and walked through to what Gwen refers to as my 'play room'. This is a room where I keep all my Liverpool memorabilia and can watch football on television without fear of interruption from Gwen, who does not appreciate football at all.

As I walked into the room I noticed that Mindy was sitting on top of my pool table, still miaowing away. As I walked towards her, I heard a noise behind me. It was a loud cracking sound. I knew that I had closed the door, so I turned around quickly.

'Oh my goodness! Mum!'

There, by the door, was the spirit of my lovely mum. She was very faint and faded quite quickly, but nonetheless, I knew that she had made her first spirit return to me.

I couldn't wait to tell Gwen, I was so excited. I had known without a shadow of a doubt that at some time my beloved mother would pay a visit to me, but I had not expected it to be so soon after her passing.

It was the end of my autumn theatre tour and many weeks after my first sighting of my mother's spirit that

I had another wonderful experience. After the last show, rather than stay overnight in a hotel, Ray, my tour manager, and I had decided to drive home. We arrived at approximately 4 a.m. As I let myself into the house I was, as usual, greeted excitedly by Jack and Penny. They had not seen me for some days and demonstrated their pleasure by jumping up and down before careering around the kitchen. Gradually they calmed down enough to allow me to make myself a cup of tea prior to retiring to bed.

It was almost 4.45 a.m. before I had finished my tea, had a chat with my dogs and enjoyed a last cigarette. I turned out the lights in the kitchen and wearily climbed the stairs.

I had not bothered to put the stair or landing lights on, as the stairs were illuminated sufficiently by a street light on the pavement outside the house. As I reached the top of them, I caught a movement out of the corner of my eye that made me turn to look along the landing towards the door of the bedroom where my mother had slept when she had stayed with us. Standing there was my mother.

I could see her very clearly. She was not, however, the tired and lined 81-year-old lady who had made her journey over to the world of spirit six months earlier, but youthful and strong, as I recalled her when I was a boy. Her hair was the dark auburn I remembered so well. She was looking at me so lovingly and then she held out her hand towards me. I realized that although she had learned how to return to visit her loved ones, she had not yet mastered voice communication.

I sent out thoughts to Sam: 'Please help her, Sam! Please, my good friend, help her!'

I so dearly wanted to hear my beloved mother's voice once more and I knew that she had always been a very determined lady and that if she could, with Sam's help, she would most certainly speak to me.

Gently, however, Sam told me that he could not do this for me. My mother had to learn at her own pace. One day soon she would achieve voice communication, but for the moment I must be happy with seeing that she was well.

Sam told me that she was very happy now, that the spirit world was a wonderful place for her and that she had met my father again. He told me that she had also been reunited with her mother, my grandmother, and that they were both so proud of my spiritual efforts.

Tears welled up in my eyes. I could feel nothing but joy at my mother's excitement at being in the spirit world.

Gradually the spirit form of my mother faded and there was nothing left to indicate that she had been there other than an enormous feeling of peace. Feeling happy and contented, I went to my bed.

The following morning I woke late. Gwen had been up and about for a few hours already. I went downstairs and happily regaled her with my experience during the early hours of the morning. We went on to discuss our plans for a forthcoming holiday break. We had decided that we would go over to our house in Spain.

Much later that evening, after we had eaten our dinner, I decided that I would go upstairs for a soak in the bath prior to retiring to bed. As I lay there relaxing in the warm foamy water, my mind drifted back to my mother and I smiled happily to myself as I remembered seeing her looking so young, fresh and healthy. After my bath, I climbed into bed and went to sleep almost immediately.

I had been asleep for some time when I suddenly woke up. I knew that a noise in the room had woken me and initially I thought that it was Gwen. Then I turned and saw that the light was not on in the bathroom adjoining our bedroom, so I knew that Gwen had not come up to bed yet and I was alone.

Suddenly there was another noise – a couple of knocking noises followed by a 'whooshing' sound. I sat up, wondering what on Earth was causing it. As my eyes adjusted to the darkness in the room, I became aware once more of the presence of my mum. Her spirit form was standing at the end of my bed.

I sent my thoughts out to her, willing her to communicate with me. She smiled the most beautiful smile and then I saw her lips moving. I heard her voice as though from a great distance. It was almost whispery in quality and I had to strain to catch what she was saying, but her eyes twinkled and danced as she knew that I was hearing her at last.

'Hiya, son. Do I look good or what?' she said.

I whispered back to her, 'You look wonderful, Mum.'

Her smile widened. She drifted up the side of my bed and I felt myself enveloped in her love. My forehead felt as though a cool hand had been pressed against it. I closed my eyes to absorb the love of my mother.

After a few moments, I felt her fading away. I opened my eyes once more, to see no more than a mere wisp of her ethereal body before she disappeared completely.

A great disappointment filled my being. Then I heard Sam's voice telling me that I could not be selfish. My mother was now in the heavenly state. She had many things to do. 'She will visit you when she can, as does your father Fred, your grandmother and all the other people who have passed from your family,' he told me.

I had already learned that this is exactly what happens. When people pass over to the higher side of life, once they have recovered from their passing they are allowed to experience many things. I could not delay my mother's progress by drawing her to me constantly with my prayers. She had my brothers and sisters and other family members to visit and there were people on the higher side of life that she would want to spend time with. Knowing my mother, there would also be a wealth of places she would wish to visit and experiences she would want to undergo before she incarnated into her next physical life.

I lay back in my bed. Once again I felt the peace and happiness that I had experienced almost 24 hours previously. I had never doubted that my mother was safe, well and with her loved ones in the spirit world, but I had craved to see her. My wish had been fulfilled, but I still could not wait until the next time my dearest mum came to call.

CHAPTER THREE

One Night in Blackpool

I had appeared at the Grand Opera House in Blackpool. After a theatre demonstration it is my practice to stay behind to sign autographs and have chats with the audience members who care to stay. On these occasions people will often approach me with fascinating tales of their experiences with the paranormal.

On this particular evening a lady who introduced herself as Margaret came up to me and told me that her whole family was being terrorized by something that was in their home. She explained that whatever it was had been there ever since she and her family had moved into the property, close on eight years previously. She told me that she was afraid and actually broke down and sobbed as she asked me whether I could help her. She pleaded with me to visit her home and attempt to remove what she described as an 'evil monster'.

I could tell immediately that Margaret was not the type of person who would exaggerate a situation, so I arranged to go to her home the following day.

I arrived shortly after breakfast time. I walked up the pathway slowly, appraising the house as I went. Arriving at the front door, I rang the bell. The door was opened by a man who said, 'Hello, Derek. I'm Andy, Margaret's husband. Please come in.'

I followed Andy through the hallway of the house and into a small but comfortable lounge, where Margaret was waiting. She invited me to sit down and offered me a hot drink.

As we sat there I noticed that Andy seemed to be very anxious and nervous. It didn't take long before he started talking about his and Margaret's experiences in the house. They had been hearing noises and small items such as car keys had been moved around their home, causing minor irritations. They had also been aware of unpleasant odours and had thought that they had a drains problem.

As Andy was speaking, I became aware of Sam standing next to me. I noticed that his presence was very strong, far more so than it would be on just a normal visit to the house of a person with a question of a spiritual nature. Intrigued by this, I opened myself up to the energies surrounding us in the room.

As I did so, I began to feel quite uncomfortable. I noticed a terrible smell, a vile stench, was beginning to permeate the air around us.

Margaret seemed aware of it too. She wrinkled her nose and asked nervously, 'Can you smell that, Derek? It happens all the time. This isn't my imagination, is it?'

I quickly reassured her that it wasn't her imagination at all. I asked her how often this happened and how long the smell remained before it subsided.

Andy answered nervously, 'About ten minutes.'

As the noxious stink spread throughout the room I noticed that the temperature had dropped rapidly. It was almost as though the front door had been left open on a very cold winter's day.

Suddenly we heard a noise. Bang! Bang! Bang! It appeared to be coming from the ceiling above us.

Margaret jumped up and grasped Andy's hand. 'Listen to that, Derek … and it gets worse too,' she whispered.

Bang, bang, bang came the noise again. It sounded almost as though someone was coming down the staircase but stamping their feet on each stair.

The noise stopped abruptly, but a moment or two later the lounge door flew open. For a few moments all was quiet, but then I became aware of a whooshing, swirling sound. Immediately afterwards I detected a male voice, barely audible to begin with but gravelly in tone. The disembodied voice gathered strength until I could hear that filthy words were being hurled into the air around us from the area around the open doorway.

Then, without any warning whatsoever, the door suddenly slammed shut. Everything went quiet and the atmosphere settled.

Margaret and Andy looked petrified and exhausted. I told them that the spirit energy in their home was a very troubled soul and that in order to discover why it was there, I would try to communicate with it.

I asked Margaret whether I could have a short walk around the house. She agreed, but told me that she did not want to accompany me upstairs.

'I haven't slept upstairs, nor has Andy, for the last eight months, especially after "that night",' she told me.

I asked her what she meant by 'that night'.

'You tell him, Andy,' she said, 'because I just can't bring myself to talk about it.'

Andy began the story. He said that Margaret had gone to bed very early one evening because she had been suffering from tonsillitis. He had been watching television in the lounge when he had suddenly heard her screaming and shouting out. He had jumped up and run up the stairs, wondering what was going on. When he reached the bedroom and opened the door, he said that it felt as though something had flown past him and out of the room. He described it as being 'like a dark mist'.

By this time Margaret had jumped out of bed and was cowering by the window, which was wide open. She was crying, the tears streaming down her face. When Andy had put his arms around her, thinking that because of her high temperature she had experienced some sort of nightmare, he had noticed that she was very, very cold indeed. She could not talk and looked petrified.

Andy explained that he had helped Margaret down to the lounge and made her a cup of tea. She had calmed down then and told him what had happened. He had been amazed.

'I still can't grasp, even today,' he told me, 'how anything like Margaret described could have gone on.'

Margaret had told Andy that she had been asleep in bed and been woken by the bed shaking and being shifted to a different angle across the room. She had then begun to feel very cold and the air around the bed had appeared to be freezing. She had heard an awful screeching sound and then she had felt as though something was attempting to smother her. The duvet had been dragged off her and she had felt as though something was touching her legs and pulling at her underwear. She said it actually felt as though somebody or something was attempting to rape her.

As Andy related this story to me, Margaret began to sob quietly to herself. 'It *was* real, Derek,' she told me. 'I didn't imagine it.'

Apparently she had also heard an awful grating voice telling her, 'I want you! I will get you!'

I absorbed this information and realized that this was a very real haunting indeed. I also realized why Sam had drawn so close to me at this time.

'Right, let's go upstairs!' I announced. I told Andy and Margaret not to worry, because Sam was close by me.

I got up from my chair and began climbing the stairs. As I approached the door that Andy indicated as their bedroom it suddenly swung open violently, banging back against the wall behind it. I heard a male voice growl to me, 'Come in, bastard! I want to see you.' This time the voice was very clear and precise.

I entered the room and walked over to the window. Immediately I detected a large energy force hovering above the dressing table. At this stage I could not see any features, but I knew that an entity was present.

I spoke out: 'Show yourself! Show yourself properly!'

A low 'Ha, ha, ha!' emanated from the energy force. Whoever it was was attempting to unnerve me.

I spoke out again: 'Why are you troubling this family?'

There was no reply.

'You shouldn't be here!' I shouted out.

Bang, bang, bang on the door was the only response. This was followed by the horrible stench I had smelled in the lounge.

As I stood by the window, the mass of energy suddenly rose up and moved across the room, heading straight for me. It hit me in my midriff with such force that it knocked me off balance. I staggered a few paces and then fell onto the bed.

Andy appeared in the doorway. 'Derek! What's happening? Are you OK?' he shouted. He reached over and helped me to get up off the bed.

We both went downstairs to Margaret and told her what had happened. I told the couple that I would like to collect my good friend Ray who accompanied me on many of the investigations that I conducted.

'When I return I'll be better equipped to deal with the matter,' I told them.

Within an hour or so Ray and I had arrived back at Andy and Margaret's house. I had quickly told him what had taken place and that there was definitely a malevolent spirit on the premises.

We knocked on the door and Andy ushered us in. I advised him and Margaret that in my opinion it would be better if they did not come upstairs with Ray and me but waited downstairs until we came back.

As Ray and I climbed the stairs, Ray mentioned that he felt a little uneasy, but I said to him, 'Come on, mate! Remember all the times we've been in situations like this. And remember that Sam's here.'

Suddenly Ray told me that he felt as though somebody had touched him on the shoulder.

'It's OK,' I told him. 'It's just Sam giving you a bit of reassurance.'

We entered the bedroom. Ray commented that he did not like the feel of the place at all. I advised him to remain quite quiet and not to say too much.

As we stood just inside the room, the door behind us slammed shut. I called out to the entity within the room: 'Show yourself! Speak out if you wish!'

Nothing happened.

I decided that I would open up and expand my aura to enable the spirit entity to use my energies to speak. I knew that this could be a dangerous thing to do because I was not sure of the strength of the spirit we were dealing with. But I also knew that without affording it this facility it was highly unlikely that we would get anything more than the gruff comments that I had received earlier. To fully understand this entity and to discover exactly why he had decided to locate himself in this house, I would need to channel his energy through my own.

As I stood in the centre of the room opening up my aura, I felt the spirit come closer to me. I moved my conscious mind and personality backwards. Closer and closer he came, until his energy was overshadowing me and being absorbed into my body. I had the impression that my body was diminishing somewhat, becoming slimmer and shorter. I spoke, but it was not my voice that issued from my mouth.

Afterwards Ray related to me what happened from this point on. The spirit entity had spoken through me. Surprisingly, he had been quite calm and reasonable at the beginning. He had spoken of his passing in a home that had been on the site of Margaret's and Andy's present house. He had given his name as James Styles and said that he had lived until he was 51 years of age. He had resided with his wife Elsa. One day he had come home early from his workplace as he had begun to feel very ill indeed. He had let himself into the house and been shocked to discover that his wife was in bed with a man with whom they had been friendly for some years.

At that point James had gone absolutely crazy with anger and grief. He had shouted and cursed and screamed. He had run at his so-called friend, grabbed him and pushed him down the stairs and out of the front door. Then he had gone back inside the house. He had called his wife filthy names and attacked her right there in the bedroom, punching her and attempting to pull her clothes away from her. He had been absolutely uncontrollable, in spite of the fact that he was only a slightly built man.

Elsa had managed to free herself from him and run down the stairs, only stopping to grab a coat before escaping through the door. James had never allowed her back into the house again.

After the events of that day James's personality had changed. He had become morose and angry. He had felt very bitter about what had happened and had decided that all women were untrustworthy and not to be respected.

A short while afterwards he had fallen ill. He recalled being in his bed and feeling burning hot. He remembered throwing off his bedclothes and not being able to breathe properly. He had contracted pneumonia. Finally, he passed away.

Upon his passing he recalled his anger and what he had done to his wife Elsa. He was now very afraid. He could not allow himself to be taken to the higher side of life completely for fear that he would be taken to a place where only bad people resided. No amount of encouragement from his guides, helpers and family members who had passed over before him could make him see that his actions had been the result of something bad being done to him, that he would be forgiven for what he had done to Elsa and that everything that had happened had been meant, as he had chosen it as part of his pathway towards soul growth. Thus James had remained in the atmosphere of his old home.

So why had the spirit of James Styles attacked Margaret? That night in the bedroom he had been reliving the moment when he had discovered Elsa being unfaithful to him. When he had pulled off the bedclothes, he had been seeing not Margaret, but Elsa. That's why he had wanted to hurt her and demean her. His anger had been enormous. It was this anger that remained in the residual energy of the house and manifested in a manner that was typical – the cold atmosphere and evil smell.

When I speak of 'residual energy', I mean energy that is comprised of memories. These memories will be of incidents that have taken place in a building, and the stronger the emotion connected with them, the stronger the residual energy left within the fabric of the building. With any building, it is also possible that there was once a structure on that site beforehand. The memory of the older building and what went on within it will still be contained in the ground upon which the newer building was erected. It is by tuning in to these residual energies that mediums are able to glean information from the past. A spirit presence, on the other hand, is when a person who has lived, worked or occupied a building in some way is drawn back to visit it once they have passed away from this physical life and on to the world of spirit beyond.

I allowed the spirit of James to recede from my energies. Ray and I went downstairs and returned to the lounge, where Andy and Margaret were waiting in trepidation for us. I imagined that they were expecting a horror story, which indeed it was, but on this occasion it was something that I could put right.

After half an hour's respite to gather my energies once more, I returned with Ray to the bedroom. This time I encouraged Margaret and Andy to accompany us.

When we reached the bedroom I asked the other three to form a circle with me and joined hands to harness our collective spiritual energies. This, together with a healthy compassion for the departed spirit of James Styles, enabled him to be collected properly by his loved ones. They were able to gently encourage him to enter his rightful place in the world of spirit and to be finally happy and at peace.

I whispered to James to look for the light and I heard him reply, in a much lighter tone this time, 'I see it, I see it!'

With his thanks echoing in my ears, I knew that he was now gone from the atmosphere and would not return. The awful events that had taken place in Margaret and Andy's home could be pushed to the past and they could now live their lives there happily and peacefully.

The next time I was in Blackpool to appear at the theatre Margaret and Andy were in the audience. After the show they waited to speak to me. They told me that from the day of my last visit there had been nothing untoward to report in their house. In fact, after a couple of weeks they had gone back to sleeping in their bedroom and had at long last been able to get a good night's sleep.

CHAPTER FOUR

A Faithful Friend

Our pets are sometimes as important to us as the humans in our lives. Be they cats, dogs, birds or hamsters, we love them all to distraction and it is heartbreaking when the day finally arrives when we have to say goodbye. The 17 years I spent with Cara, my faithful German Shepherd dog, will remain some of the most magical times of my life. I remember her with love and affection, though my grief is now somewhat tempered by the passing of time. It was a similar case with Bonnie, our younger German Shepherd, whose time with us was sadly cut short due to illness, although Gwen can still be reduced to tears when reading the wonderful poem 'Paw on the Stair' by Patricia Smith.

We now have another German Shepherd dog, Penny, and a standard poodle, whom we named Jack in memory of my great friend Jack Flavell, who was legendary in the cricketing world. Although we both adore our two 'youngsters', we will never forget Cara and Bonnie.

We are not, of course, the only people who have suffered the loss of a beloved pet. Unfortunately, because it is part of the spiritual system, there are many, many people who have suffered and who are at this moment suffering deep grief after the passing to the spirit world of their four-legged friends. Some of these people get in touch with me asking whether they will ever meet up with their pets again. Katy was one such person.

Katy lived in Loughborough. She told me that although she had never intended having a pet, as she lived in rather a small house, the situation was almost thrust upon her.

One morning as she was going out she noticed that a small gingery nondescript dog was in her front garden. She didn't take much notice of the animal because she was in quite a rush, but assumed that it was one of the many dogs who were let out on their own to take their morning walk. However, when she returned some hours later, the dog was still there. She put out a bowl of water for it and wondered whether it was lost. It was February, but the weather was particularly mild. Katy decided that she would not bother with the dog but would wait to see whether its owner came along to find it, or indeed whether it would find its way home of its own accord.

When Katy got up the next morning she looked out of the window to see that the little dog was still in her garden. It was just sitting there watching the world go by. Realizing that the little animal must be hungry and that she had no animal food in her house, she decided that she would give it some cooked meat she had left over from her meal the night before. She placed the meat into a bowl with some brown bread, opened the front door and approached the dog carefully. She was unaware of its temperament and so she was cautious. The little dog shrank away from her. She placed the bowl on the floor and retreated back inside her house. The minute her front door closed, the dog lurched forward and wolfed down the food.

This scenario was played out several times over the next couple of days. During that time Katy asked

45

around the locality in an attempt to discover whether anybody was missing their pet, but nobody knew anything about the dog. She also placed a notice in the window of her local shop and veterinary surgeon's in the hope that somebody would see it and come to claim their pet.

Over the following days the dog came to trust Katy more and allowed her to touch it. The weather took a turn for the worse and she realized that she could not leave it out in the garden. She decided that she would bring it indoors at night but let it out again in the morning. She also decided that it was now time to telephone the RSPCA in an attempt to establish whether anybody was looking for their dog. Nobody responded.

A week or more went by and a pattern was formed. Katy would bring the dog in at night and then let it out again in the morning as she went to work. Sure enough, when she arrived home each evening the little chap would be sitting on her front doorstep waiting for her.

It was as she was coming home one evening that she was stopped by a youth. 'You're the woman who's taken in a little ginger dog, aren't you?' he stated.

Katy agreed that she was, hoping that at last somebody had come forward to claim him. However, the youth's next words froze her with horror: 'You won't get anybody coming forward. The man who owned it wanted to get rid of it and tried to strangle it. He used to leave it out in all weathers and kick it too. He won't want it back because he's only interested in pedigree Jack Russells now.'

Katy thanked him for the information. In that instant she decided that the search for the owner of the dog was over: she herself would give him a home.

From that day on the pattern changed. Instead of being out in the garden during the day, the dog was given a warm bed in the kitchen. He was fed on proper dog food, not just scraps, and bought a shiny new collar and lead. He was also given a name: Hokie. The day that Hokie came to stay changed Katy's life forever.

Although Katy's parents had always owned dogs, she had never herself felt that her busy life and work schedule could accommodate a pet. She realized now that she had been wrong, because Hokie fitted in very well. Whenever she felt down, he was there to make her feel wanted and loved. When she wasn't at work, he was constantly by her side. Although he was proud to wear his lovely new collar, a lead was unnecessary, because he would follow her around, constantly keeping to her side. He was only small, but he had an enormous heart. It broke Katy's own heart to know that he had been treated so badly by his previous owner.

Of course there were times when Hokie was naughty. He had a particular liking of wood and loved to chew. It was unfortunate that the wood he chewed sometimes turned out to be Katy's skirting boards or chair legs. He was also an adroit thief. If he managed to hop out of the house without Katy knowing, he would invariably return with some booty – perhaps a carton of milk stolen from a neighbour's doorstep or even a packet of sandwiches filched from the jacket pocket or bag of some unsuspecting workman.

The years passed by and Hokie became part of Katy's life. When she got married and moved home, he was first through the door. He had long since given up his cosy bed in the kitchen and was now firmly established at the bottom of Katy's bed, and this did not change upon her marriage.

By then Katy and Hokie had been together for about 14 years. Although she had had no idea of his age when he had turned up in her life, she had assumed that he had been around 12 months old at the time. His once vibrant gingery coat was now grizzled and grey, his eyes were becoming opaque and his hearing was not all that it once had been. Nevertheless he enjoyed life and was just as eager to accompany Katy on a walk as ever.

One day, however, when Katy returned home from work she noticed a change in her old friend. He did not jump up to greet her but lay on his bed in the kitchen with his head on his paws, watching her as she moved around. There was an air about him that Katy felt was different. That evening she took him to the veterinary surgeon, who carried out some tests. A day or two later the results came through and the news was not good: Hokie had a form of cancer from which he would not recover.

Katy was devastated. She could not even think about ending Hokie's life, but she knew that it was the kindest thing to do. He was deteriorating rapidly; his breath becoming short. She vowed that she would spend one more night with Hokie and the following day she would make the ultimate personal sacrifice of sending her old friend on his way.

Hokie made the decision for her, though, as that evening he passed away in his sleep. One minute he was lying sleeping on the sofa, cuddling up to Katy as he usually did. A moment or two later, with a quick last whimper, he was gone.

The days that followed were a blur for Katy. She could not eat, nor could she sleep without the comforting weight of Hokie at her feet. She missed him so much. Her husband tried to comfort her by telling her that he would get her another dog, but she refused, telling him that nobody could replace Hokie. He had been her companion through all the trials and tribulations of the past 14 years. He had been her friend when nobody else wanted to be, he had been her companion when she had been lonely, he had smiled in his own special way with his tongue lolling out of the side of his mouth when he had known she was happy. He had even attended her wedding, wearing a smart black bow tie. She just could not countenance another dog taking his place.

Some weeks passed and Katy was at last beginning to come to terms with the loss of Hokie. She still looked for him as she opened the door when she arrived home from work every day, though, only for realization to dawn that he was not there. She still missed him terribly, but she had reached a point where she did not break down in tears each time she thought of him. It was at this point that she contacted me.

I was due to visit Loughborough and somehow Katy had heard that I was coming to a bookshop to do a signing session for one of my book releases. On the designated day, she turned up at the bookshop and waited until the end of the signing. It was at this point that she approached me and told me the story of Hokie.

'Will I ever see him again?' she pleaded with me.

I was happy to tell Katy that she would indeed meet up with Hokie once more. When her time came to pass over in to the spirit world, Hokie would run to meet her as joyfully as he had when he was here on Earth with her in his physical life. He would never forget her and the wonderful life she had given him after the awful treatment he had received from his first owner. He was her lifelong pal and this closeness would continue from beyond the veil.

Katy seemed happy to know that she would see Hokie again and that he would still be around her now, although she could not see him and had not felt his presence.

A week or two later I received an excited telephone call from Katy. 'Hokie's come back!' she told me.

She explained that she had come home from work as usual one evening and as she had opened the door she had heard a quiet 'woof' coming from the area of the kitchen. She had been surprised, as this was what Hokie had always done to greet her when she came home and she knew of course that Hokie was no longer there.

Now each evening the same thing was happening. As she opened the front door, she would hear Hokie's 'woof' in greeting. She also told me that she had definitely felt him around her in the house. She had been able to feel his presence almost as strongly as if she could see him.

The previous night had confirmed everything to her. She had been lying in bed when she had heard a patter of small paws, then felt a 'thud' as something Hokie-sized had landed on the bottom of the bed.

'I know he's back with me, Derek!' she said excitedly. 'I just know it!'

Almost six months later I was in Birmingham appearing at the Alexandra Theatre. At the end of the evening I was surprised to see Katy.

'I had to come and see you,' she told me, 'and I have to tell you that I've got a new dog. I've called her Sally and she's adorable. She'll never take Hokie's place, but I missed having a dog around the house.'

I was pleased to hear that Katy had taken the step of acquiring a new pet. It is something that I can heartily recommend from personal experience. We may love our pets to distraction, but when they go they leave a huge hole in our lives and that hole can be filled by having another pet to love. It does truly ease the pain a little and in time you get to love the new pet just as much as the pet that you lost, although in a different way.

My heart goes out to anybody who is suffering the loss of a pet at the moment. I can only say that our animals do pass over to the world of spirit, they do live on and they do come back to visit us. For anybody who would like to visit a website, I would recommend logging on to www.petloss.com. I am sure that the comfort you will receive will help you come to terms with your loss and confirm to you that your beloved pets do indeed live on.

Chapter Five

Down Memory Lane

Whilst driving from my home in Southport towards Liverpool one day I happened to take a route through Crosby, which is one of the suburbs of the city and famed for the statues of 100 men on its beach. After passing through the town I headed towards the Dock Road, the road that passes in front of the old Liverpool Dock warehouses and runs for miles through to Liverpool 8.

As I approached the beginning of the Dock Road I recalled the days of my boyhood in an area not too far away from there. I slowed down somewhat. Brasenose Road was where I had lived in the days when my mother, my older sister and brother and I had lived with my grandmother. It was in my grandmother's house that I had had my first spiritual experience when I had seen my maternal grandfather, a man who had passed to spirit before I was born. I decided that I would take a look to see what remained of the area where I spent my formative years.

As I passed the sign for Oil Salvage Limited, I turned off the Dock Road and into Marsh Lane, heading towards the Strand shopping centre. I turned right and travelled along Stanley Road, passed the High Baird College and down to Bank Hall Road, where I turned right. A short distance further along I came to the junction with Brasenose Road. My, how it had changed!

The majority of the houses with which I was familiar had disappeared now. In their place stood retail buildings. The first thing that I noticed was that the public house on the corner that I remembered as the Hanged Man – aptly named, as I recall, after the fact that a man was actually hanged on the premises – was now the Brasenose Road Café. It was open and as I had missed breakfast, I decided that I would go in and get a cup of tea and perhaps a sandwich.

The moment I walked in, I was enveloped by the smell of steaming cups of tea and coffee, toast and frying bacon. The staff in the café greeted me with 'Hello, Derek. What on Earth are you doing here?'

I explained to them that I had been driving through to Liverpool and had felt the urge to visit the area of my old home.

'Well, you sit down and I'll make you a nice cuppa and a bacon butty,' one of the women said. As I did not have much time to spare, I told her that I would take the drink and the food out to my car. 'Well you'll have to come back here and do a programme for the telly,' she said. 'We've got a ghost in here, you know!'

I was not at all surprised by her words. Although I was definitely not open to spirit activity at the time, I had already noticed that there was a huge amount of residual activity within the old building and certainly more than a suggestion that spirit people came and went between the physical world and their spiritual home.

As the woman cooked the bacon for my sandwich, she told me about the 'resident ghost'.

'We call him Jack,' she said, 'and he's a mischievous bugger! He turns taps on and off and moves things around. He makes noises all the time and follows people around the place. It can be frightening at times.

If I'm here on my own I tell him to sod off and leave me alone. He's not here all the time, though.'

I explained that he was very likely only in visitation to the old public house because he had either worked or lived there or might even have been an old customer who enjoyed revisiting the place where he had spent time during his lifetime here on Earth. I told the staff that I was not open to the spirit world at that time but that I would return at some point and find out exactly who their 'Jack' was.

I took my sandwich and cup of tea outside and climbed carefully into my car. As I sat there eating and drinking, I looked around. I noticed the opposite corner was now fenced in, with the area behind the fence appearing to contain trees. I recalled that in my days as a boy living just down the road, the piece of land had been occupied by an old building that had been bombed during the Second World War. Although part of it had remained, there had been a section where the roof had completely disappeared, leaving only two or three wooden beams remaining. There had been a huge bomb crater below this, which my friends and I used to swing over on a rope suspended from a beam. I quail now to think about what could have happened to us, but in those days we were just lads doing the things that lads do.

I remembered the cocky watchman who used to guard the other building on the site. It contained what we called 'Toby sugar'. Whilst the watchman's back was turned we would take as much of the rough brown sugar as we could, run home with it and put it into a pan to turn it into toffee. Many were the times our mothers were mystified as to how one of their once clean cooking pots had been filled with a sticky brown mess.

I finished my sandwich and turned the car around. I drove slowly down Brasenose Road looking for the exact spot where my grandmother's house had stood. The small side streets still remained, but had been terminated after about 50 yards, ending in a blank brick wall. I managed to locate my grandmother's precisely by counting the streets up from the iron bridge that still remained over a canal. The home I had loved and that had been my refuge as a child had now been replaced by a building bearing the name Bootle Car & Commercial Limited. Nothing remained to suggest that once upon a time this had been an area where people had lived in a closely knit community.

I got out of my car and walked slowly along the streets that had been so familiar to me as a young boy. I walked towards an area where St Alexander's church had once stood, with the school I had attended as a youngster next door.

I recalled the day I had 'borrowed' my aunt's new bicycle. The bike had been far too large for me, so I had had to stand on the pedals to propel it forward, my legs being far too short to actually sit on the saddle and ride it normally. I recalled hearing my grand-mother's voice shouting to me to 'Come back at once!' I had ignored her shouts, but, despite pedalling for all I was worth, I could not outstrip her. When she caught up with me I received a resounding clip around the ear and a long telling-off, not only for taking the bicycle without permission but also, even more importantly, for ignoring my grandmother. In those days I had been something of an imp and was known locally as 'Dennis the Menace' after the famous cartoon character.

I continued to stroll around, marvelling at how some places had altered so radically and yet others had remained almost the same as I remembered them. As I walked across St John's Road and under the railway bridge, I suddenly heard someone shouting my name. I turned and saw a middle-aged woman standing waving at me. From a distance I didn't recognize her, but as I drew closer her face seemed somewhat familiar. As I reached her, she gripped my hand and said, 'Derek, I thought that was you! Whatever are you doing here? You're the last person I expected to see today, but it's strange you know, because I was only thinking about you the other day.'

She introduced herself as Maggie. 'You'll remember me as Maggie Dawlish,' she said, 'but I was married for nearly 40 years to Don Petrie. You never knew him, because he wasn't from around these parts.'

Of course I remembered Maggie. She had once been very friendly with my older sister Barbara and had often played in my grandmother's house. Obviously she had changed over the years and now very much had the look of her mother. Mrs Dawlish had always been kind to us children. There'd always been the treat of a biscuit and a glass of lemonade to hand.

I told Maggie that I had been passing through the area and had felt compelled to stop and take a look around my old stamping ground. 'Isn't that strange?'

she commented. 'Here's me thinking about you and then you tell me you just felt the need to stop off around here.'

Maggie told me that her husband had passed away the previous year and as her four children had all now married, she was living alone.

'I know! Why don't you come to mine and have a cup of tea and a catch-up?' she suggested. 'I only live a minute away around the corner.'

I explained that I didn't have long to spare but would gladly accept her offer of a hot drink.

True to Maggie's word, we had walked no more than 50 yards before we were entering her neat terraced house. She had not moved far from her roots in all the years that had passed.

She ushered me into her front lounge and settled me down in an armchair set in the bay window. She then went through to the kitchen and as I heard her bustling around preparing the tea, I drank in the atmosphere of the home. There was a lovely calm and peaceful feel about the place. I knew that this had been a happy home with lots of good memories. In fact Maggie's home was just as I remembered her own mother's home – welcoming and warm. Like most of the people in the area, the Dawlish family had not had much money, but mere money could not buy the wealth of a solid family who cared about the people who lived around them.

Maggie came back through with a tray containing two mugs of tea and a sugar basin. 'We may go back a long time, but I don't know whether you take sugar or not,' she laughed.

I smiled. Still the same Maggie – the years had not changed her quick wit and jocular outlook on life.

We had been sitting for no more than 15 or 20 minutes drinking our tea when I became aware of the presence of a spirit in the room. I expanded my consciousness and opened myself up to the spirit world. I could sense that the spirit was a man and I picked up a feeling of joviality and gladness to be in the home. I immediately assumed that this was Don, the husband that Maggie had been telling me about and whom she still missed greatly.

Sure enough, a minute or so later, the spirit form of a man began to build beside the armchair in which Maggie was sitting. He was of medium height, around five foot seven or eight inches, and of stocky build. I had the distinct impression that the weight he carried had only been gained in the latter years. As a youth he had been muscular and tough. I picked up the scent and the feel of the sea, of long journeys over the rolling oceans, of hard work and long hours. The spirit man rolled up his right shirt-sleeve and pointed to the tattoo of an anchor on his arm. I realized that this was symbolic – in life he had not had such a tattoo, but it was a way of indicating to me his lifetime working at sea.

I looked at Maggie. She had always been very well aware of the work that my grandmother had done for spirit and she was also very well aware that I followed in my grandmother's footsteps. During our conversation earlier, she had said that she had heard of my office in Victoria Street and, later on, had watched me on television. 'When he was alive, I always used to brag to Don that I knew someone off the telly,' she'd told me.

Now she noticed the lull in the conversation and the fact that I had looked at her in the way that I had. 'What's up Derek?' she asked.

'You never told me what Don did for a living,' I said to her. 'Did he by any chance go away to sea? Was he away for long periods of time?'

Maggie replied that her husband had indeed spent his life going away to sea, as he had been in the merchant navy. He had worked hard to pay for a decent home for himself and his four children.

'We were always happy, though, Derek,' she said, 'I think him being away so much meant that we never got fed up with one another. He was a good man.'

Maggie smiled as she uttered the last few words. She went on to tell me that even though she was used to her husband being away so much she missed him terribly now that he had passed away. She missed the telephone calls and the letters and post cards he used to send her from everywhere his ship docked. She missed being able to share her problems with him and discuss their children.

'The kids are good to me, but it's not like having my Don,' she said sadly.

I told her that Don was with us at that moment, that he was standing beside the chair in which she was sitting.

She didn't seem surprised. 'Oh, I know,' she told me. 'I often feel him around the house, especially if there's any work going on. He might have missed overseeing things before, but he certainly doesn't miss anything now!'

I described the spirit man to her and she confirmed that it was Don.

We continued chatting for a while, with Don nodding and smiling, and then he turned and looked swiftly to his right. The spirit form of a woman was beginning to build there. I recognized her immediately. It was Maggie's mother, Ada Dawlish.

'You're mum's here, too,' I whispered to Maggie.

Her eyes filled with tears. 'I've never felt Mam around the way I do with Don,' she told me. 'I always thought I must've upset her in some way.'

I assured Maggie that this was not the case at all. Whilst some spirit people seem to forget that knowledge of their presence may frighten and disturb their loved ones still here on Earth, some are far more sensitive and do not wish to scare or upset their families. They therefore only make their presence felt in cases where they want to draw attention to themselves. This may happen if they have knowledge of an impending event to which they wish to alert their loved ones. Ada was one of the more sensitive souls. Just as in life, she wouldn't do anything to hurt people or make them afraid.

Don's spirit form faded as he made way for Ada to come centre-stage. She leaned over and kissed her daughter's cheek. As she did so, Maggie raised her hand and touched the exact spot.

'Did you feel that?' I asked.

'I did, Derek!' she exclaimed. 'Was that Mam?'

I confirmed that it was.

Maggie told me how pleased that she was to know that her mother was still around her. 'Is Dad with her?' she asked.

I shook my head. I could see Ada's lips moving and gradually I heard her faint voice. She was asking me to tell Maggie that her dad loved her just as much as she did, but that today it was impossible for him to join her on the visit to their daughter's home. She asked me to say that they were both very happy in the spirit world and that they were together. They had met up with Maggie's grandparents and her younger brother, the son that Ada had lost to spirit when he was six years old. They had also spent time with many of the people they had known – friends and neighbours – who were now resident in the world of spirit.

Ada smiled broadly and said that I was to tell Maggie that she was going to be a grandmother again. Her son Ron's wife Julie had just found out that she was expecting a baby. I was to relay the information that she would have a little girl who would be born on a Tuesday and weigh in at a healthy seven pounds.

Maggie was delighted. She told me that Ron and Julie had all but given up hope of having children. They had even been talking about adoption.

Ada asked me to assure Maggie that what she said was true and that she would find out for sure within the next couple of days. With a gleam in her eye, she then asked me to remind Maggie of something that had happened when I was a little boy.

I instantly remembered the incident she was talking about. I was around four years of age at the time. I had been playing outside with my friends when I had noticed that our next-door neighbour, Mr Boyd, was very busy at his front doorstep. He was on his hands and knees working away for a while and then he stood up and disappeared up the hallway towards the back of his house.

I wandered over to see what he had been doing and saw that he was in the process of replacing the brass cover to his front doorstep. Beside the shiny piece of brass lay a hammer and some equally shiny screws. I remembered that my grandmother had just bought a new dining table and thought how pretty the shiny screws would look fixed to the legs of the new table.

In those days a dining table was something to be proud of. It was the practice of any family lucky enough to own one to place it, folded up to its smallest capacity, against the wall of the front parlour, usually under the window. It would be covered with a velvety, tasselled cloth. The chairs to the table would be arranged strategically against the walls of the parlour. As children we were not allowed into the front parlour on our own. The room was kept for special occasions, high days and holidays or whenever somebody important like the parish priest came to call.

I picked up the hammer and screws from Mr Boyd's doorstep. I was sure that as he had stopped work, he had no need for them anymore. I went quietly in through my grandmother's open front door and crept to the parlour door, which I opened silently. I slid into the room, clutching the hammer and screws tightly. For the next few minutes I was engrossed in hammering the shiny screws into the legs of my grandmother's new dining table.

Suddenly I heard a man's voice shouting from our front door. 'Alright, alright!' I heard my grandmother's voice say as she came out of the kitchen and walked up the hallway. I heard her footsteps pass the parlour door and come to a halt at the front door.

'What's the matter, John? What's all the shouting about?' she asked Mr Boyd.

'Where's Derek?' he demanded. 'Where is he? I just nipped into the kitchen for a quick cuppa and when I came back to the step, my hammer and some brass screws had disappeared!'

My grandmother replied that I was out playing with my friends. She was unaware that at the very moment I was actually sitting in her front parlour enhancing her table legs with the missing screws.

'And anyway, John, don't come shouting here when you lose something. Derek's not to blame for everything, you know!'

With that she slammed the door and I heard her retrace her steps to the kitchen, where she and my mother had been preparing the dinner.

I sat and thought for a few minutes. From Mr Boyd's reaction I realized that I should not have used his hammer and screws without asking. I thought that the best thing to do was to tell my grandmother that I had borrowed the tools. Maybe she would come with me whilst I returned them.

I reluctantly walked down the hallway to the kitchen, dragging my feet every inch of the way. I opened the kitchen door.

My grandmother was telling my mother what had happened with Mr Boyd. 'Silly old thing,' she was saying, 'he'd lose his head if it wasn't screwed on.'

My mother was laughing along with her when she looked up and saw me standing in the doorway. It must have been obvious to her from the expression on my face that I'd been up to something.

'I hope you had nothing to do with Mr Boyd's missing hammer,' she said to me, narrowing her eyes.

Slowly I brought the hammer out from behind my back.

My grandmother closed her eyes. 'Oh no!' she said. 'And where're the screws? Did you take those as well?'

I nodded.

'Where are they?' she demanded.

I turned around, walked back down the hallway and pointed to the table legs.

My grandmother, rather than looking pleased as I had expected her to, looked stunned. My mother grabbed me by the scruff of my neck and marched me straight back to the kitchen. 'You naughty, naughty boy!' she said as she shook me.

My grandmother sighed. 'And there was me sticking up for him,' she groaned. 'I even slammed the door in John's face!'

It was a very sorry boy who, a few minutes later, stood on his next-door neighbour's doorstep. As I handed back the hammer to Mr Boyd, I muttered that I had taken his hammer and screws.

'Well, let's be having the screws then,' he said sternly.

My grandmother explained the fate of those shiny brass screws.

Mr Boyd looked stunned. 'Oh! Oh well, I'll let you take care of the punishment then,' he said grimly.

And punished I was. I was not allowed to play out for three whole days, I was sent to bed early and I had my pocket money docked in order to replace the screws I had taken from Mr Boyd's doorstep.

Maggie remembered my sorry story very well. She had been in the group of children that had been standing around the Boyds' front door listening to all that was going on.

'Oh dear, Derek!' she said. 'You were such a menace. If ever anything went wrong, you were usually in the thick of things.'

Ada was beaming and smiling. It was obvious that she loved to hear us recalling those days of over 50 years ago.

I looked at my watch. It was time for me to leave and to carry on my journey into Liverpool. I gave Maggie my telephone number and walked up the hallway to the front door. As I turned to wave her goodbye, I could see Don and Ada standing side by side behind her smiling.

As I walked to my car, I could rest happy. Although the area had changed beyond belief and many of the houses and buildings familiar to my childhood had disappeared, I was content to know that the soul of the place had not changed one iota. The spirits of the people who had been our friends and neighbours still remained.

A couple of days later Maggie telephoned me to say that Julie, her daughter-in-law, had called to tell her the good news that she was expecting a baby.

'I hope you acted surprised,' I said to her.

'Oh I did,' she replied, 'but you were wrong. The doctor said the baby's due on a Thursday.'

Some eight months went by and Maggie telephoned again. 'Julie had her baby and she weighed exactly seven pounds,' she said, 'and guess what? She was born on Tuesday, so you were right after all.'

I told her that I had not been right at all, that it was her mother who had passed on all the information.

Maggie carried on, 'D'you know, Derek, since that day when we bumped into one another, I've felt me mam around all the time as well as Don. And I can tell the difference y'know. You coming around to these parts must have been meant to happen, mustn't it?'

I agreed with Maggie. It is true that some things are indeed 'meant'.

CHAPTER SIX

A Fright in St Albans

I arrived in St Albans with Ray just after midday. After booking into our hotel we decided to go and get some lunch in the town centre. We found a suitable restaurant and went inside. Whilst we were sitting waiting for our lunch to arrive, a lady approached our table.

'Excuse me, I hope I'm not intruding, but are you Derek Acorah?' she asked.

I smiled and replied that I was indeed that person.

'I wonder whether I could have a word with you after you've finished your lunch?' the lady asked.

I agreed that after we had finished eating we would join her at her table for a cup of coffee. This we did.

The lady introduced herself as Sally and began by telling me that she lived in an old seventeenth-century house. She had bought the property about two years previously and the building had been renovated before she had moved in. She told me that it was now 'perfect' and she was very happy and proud to live there. She also said that almost from the moment she had moved into her home she had been aware that there was some sort of 'presence' in the building. She said that this hadn't bothered her at all and she hadn't been afraid, even though she was a single person living alone. It was only when she decided to undertake some renovation work outside, at the back of the property, that things had begun to go wrong.

Sally told us that the back garden was large. There was a huge lawn and beyond that there was an area where there had been some sort of outbuilding. All that remained of it now were the foundations and some rubble from the walls. Sally had asked a building company to dig out the foundations and tidy up the area so that she could extend the lawn to the back of the garden. Ever since the builders had commenced their work, though, she had noticed an unsettled feeling around her home.

'I feel as though I'm sharing the house with somebody who doesn't like me,' she explained.

After a while she had become concerned enough to ask a local priest to visit to exorcize the building. This had taken place some four months ago. She told me that the priest had said some prayers and asked that if there was a spirit person present, they would leave the home and give Sally some peace. He had blessed the house and left, telling Sally that he thought everything would be fine from that point on.

After the visit from the priest all had been quiet for a while, until one day when Sally had gone into town to do some shopping. When she had returned to her home she had been shocked. It appeared that burglars had broken into the property and ransacked the living room and kitchen areas. Ornaments had been smashed, a clock had been ripped down from the wall and her prized leather sofas had been slashed beyond repair. In the kitchen, pots and pans had been taken down and thrown onto the floor with such force that some of the tiles were cracked and broken. There was water everywhere, as though the whole room had been flooded, and foodstuffs had been taken from the refrigerator and thrown randomly onto the floor, making a terrible mess.

In a panic, Sally told me that she had run to her neighbours next door, John and Nancy. They had come in and attempted to calm her down. John had telephoned the police and they had arrived an hour or so later. They had asked Sally whether any valuables were missing. When she checked her jewellery and cash, everything was still there. No electrical or electronic equipment was missing and all her important documents were intact. In fact it was just as though someone had come into the house purely to cause devastation to the two rooms. The police could find no sign of a break-in, as all the locks and windows were untouched and undamaged. In fact Sally began to arrive at the conclusion that they were looking at her rather peculiarly – almost as though they suspected that she might have been responsible for the damage herself. They left, telling her that she would probably receive a visit from a fingerprint officer within the next day or so, but beyond that, there was nothing they could do.

Sally told me that from that day forward she had begun to hear footsteps going across her landing on a regular basis. Sometimes her television would turn itself off and then on again for no apparent reason.

Just recently she had had a visit from her niece Gemma and her daughter Hannah. This was the first time that she had ever seen Hannah and Gemma had taken some photographs of them together. When Sally had collected them after having them developed, she had been shocked to see a strange man standing with them in the photographs.

'He is not very distinct, but nonetheless he's there, standing beside Hannah and me,' she told me.

At this point she pulled out a sheaf of photographs and asked me to look at them. I took the photographs and immediately I noted the strange figure of a man, although it was slightly blurred. Next to him, and even more indistinct, was the outline of a female shape. Both of these figures were standing beside the smiling Sally and Hannah.

'You can see him, can't you, Derek?' Sally questioned me.

I told her that indeed I could – and not only that, I could also make out the outline of another person.

'D'you think that these people are anything to do with what's been going on in my home?' Sally asked me. 'Would you come and have a look around to check the place out for me?'

I explained that it was impossible for me to visit her home that day, as I was due at the theatre, but told her that I would be prepared to call the following day.

After I had completed my theatre show, I was surprised to see Sally waiting to see me in the foyer. 'I've never been to a live demonstration of mediumship before,' she told me, 'and I found it extremely interesting and very touching in parts. I now have a small understanding of the other work that you do. You're not just a ghost hunter, are you?'

We said our goodbyes after reconfirming the arrangement that I was to call at her home around noon the following day.

Over breakfast the next morning Ray and I discussed what might happen when we visited Sally's home.

'It could just be exaggeration, you know, Derek,' Ray said.

I agreed with him. There have been numerous occasions when people have approached me with horror stories but when I have investigated further I have discovered that in some cases the stories have been pure fantasy and in others there have been very logical and worldly reasons behind the 'paranormal' happenings. I told Ray, though, that on this occasion I was positive that Sally did have a spirit entity in visitation at least and that if I could, I would help her.

'I can try,' I said, 'though if the spirit doesn't want to talk to me, then there's nothing I can do about it. I can't force them to do anything they don't want to do.'

We arrived at Sally's house at the appointed time. As we pulled up outside she was waiting on the doorstep for us.

'Come in, come in,' she said. 'I have to tell you that I had a terrible night last night!'

No sooner had I walked across the threshold than I began to feel a sense of foreboding. I caught a glimpse of a slight mist appearing to drift across the hallway and up the stairs. I was sure that we were going to find out what was going on sooner rather than later!

Immediately I felt drawn towards the upper level of the house. I asked whether we could go there immediately, rather than spend time on the ground floor. Sally agreed. She ushered Ray and me towards the staircase.

As I ascended the stairs, the impressions of spirit activity grew stronger and stronger. As soon as we reached the top of the stairs I felt that I knew exactly where I should be going. I walked along the landing, stopped outside a door and threw it open.

I was not surprised to see, standing in front of me, the spirit form of a man. Although the outline was hazy and indistinct, the features of the face were very clear. Great anger seemed to emanate from this spirit being.

A sudden movement to my right made me glance in that direction. As soon as my eyesight had been drawn away from him, the spirit man made a rushing movement towards me. The expression in his eyes was terrible. The force of his spirit energy threw me backwards and I tottered back out of the room under the force of it, stumbling into Ray, who was behind me. At the same time I could hear a faint voice – a man's voice. It was as though I was listening to somebody shouting down a very long tunnel. The voice was saying, 'Leave her alone! The woman is mine!' Although the spirit man's lips were not moving, I knew that it was he who was impressing me with the words.

I regained my footing and re-entered the room. I could now see the spirit form of a woman building up. There was a great air of sadness about her. She appeared to be sobbing and in terrible distress.

Then I heard Sam's voice. He was telling me, 'Help her, Derek. The young girl needs to be shown the light in order to gain the peace she has earned.'

I looked towards the female spirit. Her face bore an expression of pleading. She spoke to me: 'Please, please help me. I'm trapped here where I don't belong. I was brought here against my will and I was hurt. Please help me!'

If I was to help this young woman in spirit, I needed to remove myself from the atmosphere of the room for a brief period to gather my spiritual protection around me. If I were to remain in the atmosphere of such venom and hatred, I knew I would not be able to help at all.

I descended the stairs and stood by the front door for a few moments. As I did so I pondered the spiritual dilemma into which I had been placed. Sam had given me no information about the background of the two spirit people and I felt that I needed to offer the male spirit a chance to explain himself.

After a while, I felt that it was time to go back up the stairs to see what could be done to help the situation. I was aware that it was of paramount importance to help not one but both of these lost spirits.

I advised Sally of my intentions.

'D'you think you will be able to help them, Derek?' she asked.

'I certainly hope so,' was my reply.

I suggested to Ray that he accompany me upstairs but I felt that it would be better if Sally remained downstairs. I was not sure just how strong a spirit the man in the bedroom was.

We entered the room once more. The male spirit was still standing there. He was more distinct now. His anger did not appear to have abated or diminished in any way whatsoever. I attempted communication with him, explaining to him what my intentions were, but he remained silent.

Then I hit upon the idea that I could invite him to come forward and use my voice to give substance to his thoughts and intentions and to enable us to understand what had happened to him. I spoke once more to him and invited him to come closer to my aura.

He continued to glare balefully at me and I heard Sam's voice warning me not to allow him too close to me.

I knew that Sam was protecting me, but I felt the need to know the reason behind the anger and bitterness of this spirit soul. 'After all,' I reasoned to myself, 'I have free will. I don't have to do everything that Sam tells me!'

Suddenly, without warning, the man's spirit energy whooshed towards me. I allowed him to enter my auric field, absorbing his energies as I did so. I felt as though I was growing in girth, although my height remained the same, and that my hands and feet had swelled to larger proportions. This was not a comfortable feeling at all. The spiritual presence so close to me was abhorrent to me.

'Jacob welcomes you!' said a voice, followed by a particularly evil laugh.

I immediately knew the details of Jacob's life. He had been a businessman running a corn merchant's shop locally. He liked nothing better than to drink heavily and was detested by others because of his meanness and cruelty. He respected nobody and hated women, but used them at will.

As I stood there, I began to take on the feeling of having drunk an awful lot of alcohol. I felt angry and wanted to lash out at somebody. I felt a deep dislike for everything and everyone around me.

I turned to look to the other side of the room. The young girl was still there. She was now cowering in a corner. I felt as though I had a memory of something and my anger grew as I tried to recall what it was. Suddenly I knew. Jacob had paid for the young woman to accompany him home, but unfortunately she had not rendered the services for which he had paid.

I then became a little confused. From Jacob's energies I realized that I was not in fact in his home. That had been located elsewhere – no more than 100 yards away at the bottom of the garden. I realized that the derelict building that Sally was intending to do away with completely was in fact Jacob's home.

Jacob's anger grew and grew. 'I'll strangle her, the bitch!' he roared. 'Cheating me of my hard-earned money!'

With that I felt his energy suddenly engulf me completely and I almost ran towards the spirit form of the young woman as she grovelled close to the floor. With the last vestiges of my own consciousness I realized that I was hosting a violent and hostile spirit.

My next recollection was Ray's voice. 'Derek! Derek!' he shouted. 'Come on, Derek! Come forward!'

Gradually I groped my way back to consciousness. I was half-lying on the floor of the room and Ray was shaking me.

'Oh, Ray,' I said, 'I was taken unawares with that one.'

Then I heard Sam's voice again. It did not have the peaceful and calm tone in which he usually addressed me. Sam was angry. I had ignored his warning and used my free will, with the direst consequences. I had arrogantly assumed that I could deal with the situation in spite of Sam's words of caution. I had taken for granted that he would protect me come what may.

I scrambled to my feet. I mentally apologized to Sam, who bowed his head towards me in acknowledgement. Poor long-suffering Sam – I am indeed a trial to this great spirit being.

I turned to Ray. 'Let's go downstairs and explain to Sally what's happened,' I suggested.

We returned to the lounge, where Sally was waiting for us. She looked nervous as we opened the door and walked in. I explained the reason for the noise and the shouting.

When I had finished speaking, she looked very agitated. 'So that means that I have an evil spirit in my home?' she asked. 'How can I continue living here in those circumstances?'

I knew that to clear the atmosphere I needed help. 'Do you know of any mediums living locally?' I asked Sally.

She told me that she knew of a couple who lived quite close who were both Spiritualists, although she was unsure whether they were mediums or not. They were friends of a friend of hers and she could contact them by telephone if I wished. I thought that at least these two people would have some knowledge of the workings of spirit and so might be able to help.

Sally made the telephone call. Half an hour later the doorbell rang and the couple walked in. Sally introduced me to them. Their names were Peter and Audrey. I could feel immediately that they were people of strong spiritual belief. Their energies were clear and their strength of spirit was just what I needed. They told me that although they did not practise as mediums, they were both members of a rescue circle at the local Spiritualist church. A rescue circle is a group of mediums who have gathered together. Their aim is to send out loving thoughts to any spirit entity who may not have progressed fully to the world of spirit and achieved their rightful place on the higher side of life. The mediums will encourage the lost spirit to proceed towards the light of the world beyond rather than remain in the atmosphere of the physical world.

I realized that spiritual inspiration had brought these people to Sally's mind when I had asked about a local medium. I explained the situation to them and they immediately agreed to help me clear Sally's home of her unwanted visitors. We agreed that our first endeavour would be to rescue the young spirit girl and send her to the light. We would then deal with Jacob.

All of us ascended the stairs to the bedroom. Sally could hardly speak, she was so nervous. I gently told her that if she did not want to, she did not have to remain in the room.

'No,' she said. 'I want to help do this. I want to see an end to all that has been going on and have a peaceful home.'

We all gathered round in a circle and joined hands. As we concentrated collectively I felt the positive ener-gies begin to grow and expand. I was aware of Sam's presence, together with that of the highly evolved souls in guidance to Peter and Audrey. I uttered a prayer of protection, asking that the white light of spirit surround us and guard us. I knew that Peter and Audrey were adding their words to mine. After some minutes I decided that it was time to begin.

We prayed to the higher side of life, asking that the guides and loved ones of the lost girl come to collect her, to show her the way out of the limbo she had remained in for so long. All the while we prayed, the glowering spirit of Jacob remained in the room, shuffling and periodically banging on surfaces.

Gradually, I became aware of a bright light, almost as though a darkened window had been opened onto a sunshiny world. A shaft of illumination seemed to shine down. I heard Audrey gasp, then I saw the spirit of the young girl appear to dissolve into the shaft of light. I knew that she had been recovered by her loved ones. A moment or two later, the light dimmed. She was safely on her way to the higher side of life.

It was time now to deal with Jacob. We all continued to pray. I could detect that he was very uncomfortable. He did not want to go. He was afraid – afraid of facing the consequences of his actions during his time here on Earth.

As the strength of our prayers increased, I was aware of Jacob rushing towards me in an attempt to enter my auric field once more, but I repulsed him. In the face of Sam and the legion of spirit souls in the room protecting our little group, he was not strong enough. I could feel his presence weakening dramatically. I called upon the higher side of life to collect this wretched soul and take him to a place where he could begin his progression towards salvation.

Gradually, I could feel the atmosphere clearing. I knew that our mission had been accomplished. Jacob was gone from Sally's home forever.

We returned downstairs to enjoy a hot drink and I thanked Peter and Audrey profusely for their help.

'We were very pleased to be able to assist you, Derek,' Peter said. 'It was meant to be!' And he was right.

I was able to assure Sally that her home was now free of malevolent spirits. She could live there happily without fear of disruption.

CHAPTER SEVEN

Liverpool, Capital of Culture

This year, 2008, sees Liverpool celebrating its year as 'capital of culture'. I am exceedingly proud that my home city has been chosen for this honour. Recently, work has been undertaken to improve the city centre and many changes have been made to the 'old Liverpool' that I knew as a boy and spent time in both as a youth and a man. Buildings have been razed and others refurbished. My old office space in Victoria Street has now been converted into luxury apartments. The whole place has been cleaned and uplifted and is rapidly becoming once more a city to be proud of, a place people will enjoy visiting.

The popular perception of Liverpool over the years has not been particularly good and it is true that for a while after the downgrading of the city as a port and thus the loss of one of its major industries, it was left to deteriorate. But how times have changed! The city centre is now a vibrant and cosmopolitan shopping area boasting designer outlets as well as the regular high-street shopping opportunities, and smart cafés and restaurants are available in place of the 'greasy spoon' culture that once dominated the eating-out experience in the city.

Liverpool has a long and colourful history and the city and its outlying suburbs can be fascinating places to visit. Many of the sites of interest are virtually unknown to people other than residents of the city. Over the years I have been astounded myself at some of the secrets that have been unearthed in the area. To anybody with a couple of days to spare, I would defi-nitely recommend a trip to Liverpool. From the Pier Head to the outer reaches of Speke and Hale Village in the south and up through to Sefton in the north, you won't be disappointed.

Of course it is not only the architecture and historical detail that is fascinating to both visitors and Liverpudlians. The whole of the city and its surround-ing area is exceedingly haunted. Tom Slemen, a local author and radio personality, has written numerous books covering the ghostly goings-on of Liverpool in his 'Haunted Liverpool' series. I was unaware myself of the numerous haunted locations until I met Tom a number of years ago, when he took me to Penny Lane and Rodney Street. An account of the discoveries we made can be found in my book *The Psychic Adventures of Derek Acorah*.

Now I would like to relate to you a few other experiences I have had during my travels around my home town.

WAVERTREE

Although it is many a long year since I visited the Liverpool 15 district, I still hold the place in very high regard. It was here that I had my first 'shop' opposite the police station on Wavertree Road. Every morning at 10 a.m. I opened the doors and gave readings to people who called in. It was not very long before I became inundated with people wanting to see me. As a result I had to install a diary system whereby anybody who wanted to have a reading with me would telephone or call in and make an appointment in advance. It saved having a very crowded waiting room and people did not have to sit for hours queuing up.

I look back on those days with fondness. The people of Wavertree were warm and welcoming. They may not have had much, but they were wonderful to me.

It was at that time that I became the proud owner of Cara, the German Shepherd dog who stayed with me for nigh on 17 years. Cara became very well known, but not always for the right reasons. She used to curl up at my feet under the desk at which I sat. The person who had come for a reading would sit opposite me and would mostly be unaware that there was a dog in the room. On most occasions Cara would be very good and would keep quiet. In fact she spent most of her time sleeping. That situation would change, however, if the person sitting opposite me had visited the shops, especially the butcher's, before calling in for their appointment with me. On more than one occasion I had to pay to replace the sausages or hamburgers that Cara had silently stolen from the shopping bag that had been placed on the floor next to her.

Eventually Cara and I moved on, but my memories of Wavertree still remain. I had not had occasion to visit that part of the city again, though, until just recently, when I was contacted by a gentleman who wished to discuss a business idea with me. He was based in the Childwall area of Liverpool, which is literally next door to Wavertree. As I was travelling from Liverpool city centre, my natural route to Childwall lay through Liverpool 15.

The section of Wavertree Road in which I had my shop all those years ago has changed to some degree. As I drove further down past Edge Hill station and towards Wavertree High Street, though, everything was the same as ever. It had not altered one jot.

I parked my car in a side street. I just felt that I would like to look around and refresh my old memories. There was the Cock & Bottle public house, now incorporating what had once been the smallest house in Britain. A little further down the High Street was the Lamb Hotel, another old public house, and opposite was Balusters, one of the quaintest shops in the area with its original Georgian bow-front.

I glanced to my left, towards Picton clock, to check the time. I still had quite a while before my appointment, so I walked towards a small octagonal building I had often noticed as I had driven by many years before. I hadn't a clue what it was.

Standing in the midst of a clump of trees and surrounded by a grassed area, the building was constructed of what looked to me to be old sandstone and had what I would call a steepled roof. Its windows were bricked up and the doorway was locked with a huge padlock.

I walked around this strange building, still none the wiser as to what it would have been. I could see that it had had a row of windows up under the line of the roof. These were now partially blocked with sandstone, but I caught a glimpse of the bars that had at one time covered them.

'You're not going to investigate the old lock-up, are you?' I heard a man shout over to me.

I turned and looked round. A middle-aged chap was walking towards me, smiling. 'Hello, Derek,' he said, and repeated his question.

I told him that I wasn't conducting any investigations at the moment, that I was just passing through and had always wondered what the building was, though this was the first opportunity I had ever had to stop and take a look.

The man, who introduced himself to me as Terry, told me that he lived in the area and that Wavertree had once been viewed as a village. At that time it had been on the outskirts of Liverpool. What I was presently standing on was what was left of the village green, and if I had any cows or other livestock, I would be able to graze them there because it was the only surviving piece of common land in the city. I looked around me at the tiny grassed area. There wouldn't be many cows or goats getting fat on the yield of this particular plot!

Terry went on to tell me that the building I was looking at was a lock-up. In the eighteenth century, if Wavertree's sheriff deemed it necessary, this was where the drunk and disorderly would be locked up for the night. I thought to myself that there couldn't have been many people drunk and disorderly on any given night in those days, because the building was tiny!

As I stood next to the small building, I could not help but notice that there seemed to be an air of sadness around the place, something of a desperate feeling. I was not open to the world of spirit at that moment, but mentioned my feelings to Terry.

'I don't understand that, Derek,' he said. 'As far as I know, it was only used to house people for the night who'd overstepped the mark in the drinks department.'

I was bemused at that because I definitely felt that there was something more than bad hangovers in the residual energy there. I turned to thank Terry and wish him goodbye.

'If you give me a telephone number, I'll take a look in the library and let you know whether I find anything,' he told me.

I handed over my contact number, thanked him once more and wandered away across the road. An old black-and-white house opposite Picton clock had caught my eye.

As I crossed the busy road onto the roundabout, I stopped briefly to read the inscription on the clock tower – 'Time wasted is existence; used is life' – and mused on how true that saying was.

I noticed, as I got nearer, that the black-and-white building housed a funeral director's. I thought it was a pity that one of the most attractive houses in the neighbourhood was not being enjoyed as a family home.

On I went around the corner and spied yet another hostelry. This time it was the Coffee House. I looked back at the clock. I still had a good bit of time to kill before my meeting, so I decided to go inside and enquire whether the landlord could supply me with a cup of tea or coffee. I had noticed that the sale of food was advertised outside and so I thought it was likely that my request would be met.

As I walked in through the front door I was amazed at the size of the place. Towards the front of the public house it was almost like a library, with shelves full of books, lots of carved woodwork and a large fireplace. The ceiling was intricate in its design and the bar stretched through the whole of the front part of the building. The rear opened out to a dining area which was raised at the end and could be reached by two or three steps.

It was around 2 o'clock in the afternoon and so very quiet in the pub. The person attending the bar happily supplied me with a cup of coffee, which I carried to a table towards the back of the huge room.

As I relaxed with my coffee, I looked around at the old photographs and prints on the walls and wondered about the history of the place. I would not have been at all surprised if at one time it had been a bank or some kind of official building, though in all the time I had been living in and travelling to Wavertree, the Coffee House had been nothing other than a public house.

As I looked towards the fireplace I became aware of the spirit presence of a slim dark-haired young woman. She appeared to be looking for someone. I had the definite impression that she had lost her life to influenza or some illness of that sort. I was certain that she had had strong ties with the building in times gone by. I was also just as certain that she only visited from time to time; she was certainly not grounded in the area.

Another spirit person then materialized to the left of the fireplace. I felt that something untoward had happened in that area – somebody had collapsed and died. I was given the name 'William' and then a surname 'Dunne'. I felt sure that whatever had happened to this man had taken place in the late 1800s, certainly no later than the very early 1900s.

Next, the spirit of a dark dog appeared around the corner of the bar. It was a large breed such as a Rottweiler or a Doberman – I wasn't sure which, because I only got the briefest of glimpses. For the spirit of a dog to come back to a building, it must have at one time been connected with it in some way. Perhaps it was the beloved pet of a former landlord or perhaps its owner had been a frequent customer of the public house. Because those particular breeds of dog are only of recent popularity, I did not feel that it would have dated back very long at all.

A movement a little further down the room caused me to turn. I knew it was not a member of the bar staff who had come out from behind the counter, because the two or three people who were on duty at the time were busying themselves clearing behind the bar, as there were no customers to serve. I looked hard and, as I did so, the spirit form of a man began to build. He was a rough-looking and unkempt individual with longish hair. He was probably in his forties when he passed to the spirit world, but as he was presenting to me he looked quite a few years older. I knew that he had been employed in some capacity around the building. I also knew that although he visited the public house quite frequently he was not a grounded spirit and was merely calling in through memory. I doubt very much whether he would have been viewing the building as it is today; he would have been more likely to have been going back to a time around the middle to late 1800s.

I began to feel an atmosphere of business and bustling, of groups of people gathering. I was impressed by the names 'Amy' and 'Robert'. There were different age groups, all chattering away in family groups. They seemed to be waiting for something. One or two of the men appeared to be the worse for drink and I wondered whether they would have been on their way to the lock-up across the road if the local sheriff had come along. I knew that the rough-looking man I had just seen had somehow been connected with these people during his employment and wondered whether the place had once been a coaching house of sorts.

I glanced at my watch and reluctantly noticed that it was time for me to return to my car and make my way to my meeting. I had enjoyed wandering around that small area of Wavertree. I had discovered places that I did not know existed and vowed that some day I would return, maybe to conduct an investigation.

A week or so after my brief visit to Wavertree I received a telephone call. At first I didn't recognize the voice when the man introduced himself as Terry.

'You remember, Derek,' he said. 'I met you in Wavertree by Picton clock. I told you I'd give you a ring if I found out more about the lock-up.'

Of course I remembered. I was interested to hear whether Terry had discovered any more information about the small building in the middle of Wavertree Green.

Terry proceeded to tell me that he had visited the local library and had also talked to several people who were knowledgeable about Wavertree and the surrounding area.

'You were right, Derek,' he said. 'That building wasn't just used to keep people overnight.'

Apparently in the early 1800s the small octagonal building had been used as a temporary mortuary when there had been a cholera epidemic in the locality. A little later it had also been used to house people coming over from Ireland to escape the potato famine. They were desperate for a roof over their heads and as there was no other form of shelter, they had used this small building.

'Thank you so much, Terry,' I enthused. 'I just knew that there was more to that building than a temporary prison.'

'Well, you were right when you said that people there would have been sad and desperate,' replied Terry.

He went on to tell me a little more about the area. I was interested to hear that the Coffee House public house had once upon a time been a depot for the horse trams that ran between Wavertree and the city. No wonder I had received psychic impressions of people gathering in family groups and the scruffy ostler.

I was so grateful to Terry. It is most frustrating when I receive information psychically, because there is no method of checking whether I am correct. If I have communication with a spirit person, either directly or via my spirit guide Sam, then I will never question that – my trust is absolute. However, when a medium is psychically tuned in to an area or a location, mistakes can be made, especially when the building is as well used as a public house. The masses of vibrations from the large numbers of people over the years dilute the energies from older times.

It was at the end of my conversation with Terry that he asked me a question: 'Derek, I know that it's quite cheeky of me to ask, but could you do something for me?'

I had more than an inkling as to what that request would entail. 'Of course I will,' I replied. 'What would you like me to do?'

Terry asked me whether I could do a reading for him. Of course I was happy to oblige. We arranged a date a couple of days ahead, when I was free for an afternoon, and I agreed to call at his home.

On the appointed day I arrived at Terry's house. As I opened up to his vibrations, I was almost immediately aware of a spirit woman building up next to him. She appeared to be quite young – in her twenties, I suppose – and she told me that her name was Sharon. Then she confirmed that she had only been 24 years of age when she had passed over to the world of spirit.

I told Terry that I had immediately connected with a young woman and passed on the information that she had given me. His eyes lit up and filled with tears. He let out a huge gasp: 'It's our Sharon – my sister, who passed over 10 years ago August gone! That's exactly who I wanted you to contact for me.'

I conversed with Sharon about the cause of her passing and she told me that it had been due to breast cancer. She said that she was 'alright now' and to tell Terry that she was with her dad Paddy, who was also in spirit.

Terry laughed. 'Oh, she'll be alright with me old man to look after her,' he said.

He started to talk about Paddy, and Sharon butted in, laughing, and told me that I should tell Terry that Paddy was 'stone cold sober these days'.

Terry chuckled. 'Oh dear! He loved his drink, Derek. Me mam had some right old days with him!'

Sharon began to talk about 'Vera's varicose vein operation' and said, 'Her legs look lovely now.'

When I related this, Terry's face was an absolute picture. 'Vera's our mam. She had the operation about four months ago, and yes, she is made up with the result.'

Sharon went on to say that they were not a church-going family, but now, whilst in spirit, she hoped that 'Mam and our Terry and other family members' would take stock and think about God and his workings.

The reading drew to an end. Terry could not stop thanking me, telling me that he couldn't wait to go and see his mam and tell her all that had been said.

'You don't know what you've done for me, Derek,' he said to me. 'I've been wondering and worrying about our Sharon ever since we lost her. It was a terrible time and I just couldn't get to grips with the idea that any God who was worth his salt would let a lovely young lass like Sharon go through what she did.'

I explained to Terry that, difficult though it might be to come to terms with, it is my belief that before we enter our physical lives we choose the way in which we will live those lives. We choose the burdens we will have to carry, the things we will have to endure and also the manner of our passing back to the world of spirit. So it would have been with Sharon.

Terry nodded. 'It *is* a difficult thing to come to terms with, Derek,' he said, 'but I know through what you've done today that our Sharon's happy and well – and what's more, she's with me dad!'

GATEACRE

Gwen and I were travelling back home after dropping a family member off at Speke airport. We had come down through Garston and Woolton, fascinating places in their own right, when Gwen asked me whether I would like to see where she had spent her early childhood. I agreed, but suggested that we stop off for lunch before we did so. 'I know the very place,' said Gwen.

We drove out of Woolton and down a hill towards Gateacre. As we reached the crossroads at the bottom of the hill Gwen told me to turn left and park up in the car park of a beautiful old black-and-white establishment.

The Black Bull was the name on the post that stood in the cobbled area at the front of the building.

Before we went to eat Gwen and I walked around the corner, where she showed me what was once her old school. 'It's just as I remember it. It hasn't changed a bit,' she said.

Actually it had changed a bit, because it had been converted into apartments – the fate of many of the old buildings in and around Liverpool. But the building had, Gwen assured me, remained the same, apart from the playground at the front. The wall had now been lowered and the entrance centralized rather than being at the far left-hand side.

As we walked back towards the Black Bull, Gwen pointed out to me the row of cottages where many of her friends had lived and the old butcher's shop, now a funeral director's establishment.

Next to the Black Bull were two black-and-white houses. 'They used to be the post office and a chemist's shop!' exclaimed Gwen. 'I can recall my mother hooking the handle of my pram over one of the bollards in front of them to prevent it rolling down the hill with me in it!' she laughed. 'And across there,' she pointed across the road, 'is what was once a grocer's shop. I can remember Mr Bostead weighing out the sugar and the butter and putting mixed biscuits from glass-fronted tins into a brown paper bag.'

I could see that Gwen was enjoying reliving her memories, but I reminded her that we really should eat some lunch.

We entered the Black Bull. It was surprisingly modern inside. It didn't take long, though, for Gwen to be off talking about her memories again.

'I worked here for a while many years ago,' she laughed. 'It's changed dramatically since those days, though.'

Gwen went on to describe the building as it had been almost 40 years ago. The section we were sitting in was new. It was modern and pleasant, I have to say. The older part, the part that Gwen remembered working in, was now a serving area and not open to the public. The old wooden fretwork still remained and seemed rather at odds with the new smooth-walled part with its modern open-sided fire.

We ordered some food and sat gazing reflectively into the flames. I was sure that this had once been some kind of coaching inn. I was also sure that the part of the establishment in which we were now sitting had once been outdoors. I had the distinct impression of a yard with horses' hooves clashing against the cobbles, jingling harnesses and people hurrying and scurrying.

'Do you know anything of the history of the place?' I asked Gwen.

She shook her head. 'I don't. I'm sorry,' she replied.

I told her about hearing the sound of horses.

'There used to be a riding stables at the back, but it's now been turned into mews cottages, I noticed,' Gwen replied.

No, that wasn't the type of equestrian activity being shown to me. The impressions that I was receiving were definitely involved with this particular building and not the locality.

Our food arrived, and delicious it was too. As we spent time over coffee I received further impressions. There was a definite Scottish influence. Somebody who had been in charge of the public house at some time had strong Scottish links and a seafaring background. I could see people in my mind's eye rushing and scurrying during the darker hours bringing in goods that had come from ships. I was aware of some form of illicit trading – trading to which the local bobby had turned a blind eye. I was sure that at some time ladies of the night had also been brought to the premises on a regular basis. They had been transported by carriage from the centre of Liverpool. It had all been arranged by the Scotsman who had headed the establishment. I heard a faint whisper of the name 'Donald' or 'Donaldson'.

I drifted further back in time and more impressions came crowding in. Impressions of gatherings of people and even hangings filled my mind. I could see a village green and a large tree with an ominous swinging rope. I wondered how old the building we were sitting in was and whether there had been something there before it. I promised myself that I would find out – for my own satisfaction, if nothing else.

It was time to go. We continued our journey up Belle Vale Road with Gwen pointing out along the way the church where she had been christened and telling me that when she was a young child, the area had been fields. Now it was covered in houses. Gwen recalled the prefabs from the post-war period.

We reached the traffic lights at Childwall Valley Road and turned right and then almost immediately left into Naylor's Road.

'This is where I lived,' Gwen told me, 'although the house no longer exists. There was a farm here with two shire horses, Blackie and Duke. One day they escaped from their field and careered up and down the road! We lived at Naylorsfield – it was a market garden at the time.'

She scowled and muttered darkly that she would never forgive Liverpool Corporation for building a particularly nasty housing estate on the land and naming it Naylorsfield. Now, thankfully, those very utilitarian houses have disappeared and pleasant modern homes have been built in their stead.

And so we continued along the road and through to the M57 and home, but I made a mental note to return to Gateacre. With its gazebo, its old cottages and a number of very old public houses, it is a fascinating place and I would very much like to explore it further.

CHAPTER EIGHT

A Poltergeist in Hastings

Ray and I were in Hastings, where I was appearing at the White Rock Theatre for two nights. We had been away from home for five days and were both looking forward to travelling back up north after the second show in order to enjoy a couple of days in our own homes before continuing with that season's theatre tour.

The first show was completed and I was tired as we headed back towards our hotel. After a quick cup of tea we both retired to our bedrooms for a shower and a good night's sleep.

As we parted company at the door of my bedroom, Ray handed me a bundle of letters. At every theatre I visit I find that people have written to me care of the theatre. When these letters are passed on to Ray, he hands them to me after the show so that I can read them when I am relaxed, without the prospect of work ahead of me.

After I had showered, just before I was about to climb into bed, I noticed the unopened letters lying where I had left them on the table. Normally I would wait until the morning before reading them, but as I did not feel quite ready for sleep I decided that I would open one or two and read them then.

The first few letters were from people who had written to me thanking me for messages received at previous theatre demonstrations. Still more congratulated me on the success of my latest television programme, *Paranormal Egypt*, and one or two asked me to contact them because they needed my help with regard to questions they had concerning the paranormal. It was the fourth such letter that made me sit up and vow that as soon as possible I would get in touch with the person who had sent it.

The following morning I discussed the letter with Ray over breakfast. It had described 'evil spirits' causing problems in what had once been a peaceful and happy home. There had been scratching and banging noises, a sound as though wind was blowing from behind a bedroom door and disgusting smells lingering in the atmosphere. I informed Ray that I intended contacting the person who had written it right after breakfast.

'Are you sure, Ackers?' he said. 'You and I know that sometimes people do exaggerate things.'

I was convinced that the letter contained a genuine cry for help and so I told Ray that I was definitely going to pursue the matter.

I telephoned the lady who had written the letter. She had signed herself 'Mrs D. Scott'. When she answered the telephone, at first she registered surprise but then told me that she was overjoyed that I had decided to get in touch. 'And do call me Delia,' she said.

She seemed to be a very nice and calm sort of soul. Briefly, she outlined once more the contents of her letter. 'Do you think you can help, Mr Acorah?' she asked at the end of her story.

'I think I may be able to,' I said, 'and please call me Derek!'

Delia gave me her address and brief directions to her home. I told her that Ray and I would be with her in an hour or so.

* * *

Delia's home was large and obviously expensive. Before we had reached the front door it was opened by Delia herself. She was a middle-aged woman who obviously took care of herself. Her hair was neatly styled and she was dressed in smart trousers and a sweater. She certainly didn't look to me to be the type of person given to flights of fancy.

As Ray and I entered the hallway, even before I had opened myself up to the atmosphere of the house, I began to feel very hot and agitated. Then, just as quickly, I felt a temperature drop and became quite chilled. This coolness was maintained as we walked down the hallway.

'Is your home always this cold?' I asked Delia.

She told me that all the time she and her husband, who was presently away on business, had been living in the house, they had had a problem keeping it warm.

'It doesn't matter what amount of heating we have on, it's always cold now,' she said.

She ushered Ray and me into a sitting room which contained a beautiful inglenook fireplace. As we sat down in the armchairs in front of it, I had the distinct feeling that something wished to remain hidden and secret. There was a sense of intrigue. I began to feel unsettled.

I turned to Delia. 'If what you have told me about the events taking place in your home is accurate, why haven't you contacted a medium, a priest or someone else who could attempt to help you with the problem before now?'

She replied that she hadn't really noticed anything happening until approximately three months ago, when her young grandson Charlie had come to live with her. It had been after that that things had built up to the point where she felt that she could no longer cope.

'I have watched you over the years on the television, and even more so just lately,' she continued, 'and so I thought I would wait until you were in the area and that's why I contacted you. I know that you're the man who'll be able to help me.'

Delia explained that the family had suffered an awful tragedy in that her daughter Rebecca had passed over to the world of spirit as the result of unexpected heart failure at the age of 28. Her former husband had deserted her and Charlie two or three years previously and unfortunately had not kept in close contact with them. When he had learned of his ex-wife's death and the plight of his son, he had not wanted anything to do with bringing him up. He was willing to support the boy financially but, having married for a second time, he did not feel that he wanted to disrupt his life by bringing a child from a previous relationship into his home. It had been a natural step for Delia and her husband to offer their grandson a home.

'It's so sad,' she had written in her letter. 'Nobody wanted him but us, but every day since he's been here, the disruptions have built up more and more. I'm at my wits' end and just don't know what to do.'

I asked Delia what time Charlie was expected back from school. She told me that he would be home around 3.30 p.m. Then I asked how he was coping since losing his mother.

'He's a very quiet boy and doesn't have much to say really to either me or his grandfather,' she told me. 'I try to speak to him about his mother, but he doesn't really want to talk. He's doing well at school now. There was an initial wobble after we lost Becky, but he seems to have settled down again now.'

I began to think that I could have the answer to the problem. I asked whether it would be possible to go up to Charlie's bedroom before he arrived home from school.

Delia looked surprised that I would ask to see her grandson's bedroom first. 'I thought you'd be wanting to delve around the attics and cellars!' she laughed.

I explained that I had a hunch that there was a link between what was going on in her home and her grandson's emotional turmoil upon losing his mother – turmoil that he was keeping suppressed. Being of a quiet nature, not feeling able to speak to his grandmother, grandfather or teacher and without his father to turn to, poor Charlie was keeping his suffering to himself.

Delia led the way to Charlie's bedroom. It was decorated in the typical fashion of a boy's room. I noticed that although it was tidy, one or two items were still strewn around where Charlie had obviously left them that morning.

I walked a few paces into the room and opened myself up to the atmosphere. It felt uneasy and unsettled. There was tension in the room and I felt my nerves begin to jangle. I was turning around to look at Delia and Ray, who were standing in the doorway, when suddenly there was a loud bang.

'Watch out, Derek!' Ray shouted. 'The end of that bed just lifted up and dropped down again.'

Delia was clutching onto Ray's arm, her eyes round and wide with shock. 'If I hadn't seen it with my own eyes, I wouldn't have believed it!' she gasped.

It was now almost three o'clock. I decided that the best thing to do was to go downstairs and await Charlie's return from school. If my theory was correct, it was more than likely that further disruption would be experienced upon his return. We retreated back down the stairs to await his homecoming.

I knew with certainty that the problem I was dealing with here was poltergeistal activity. There weren't any 'evil spirits' in the house, as Delia had feared.

Poltergeistal activity is commonly linked to children who are approaching puberty or who have undergone emotional unrest of some kind. It is more prevalent with those who have previously exhibited signs of psychic ability. It is generally agreed that a poltergeist is not the manifestation of a spirit person but rather an abundance of energy generated by and drawn to adolescents or children suffering severe emotional stress.

Usually poltergeistal activity is limited to noises, i.e. rustlings, tappings, knocks and dragging sounds, but occasionally items can be thrown, furniture moved and noxious smells created. In extreme cases there have been reports of poltergeistal energy causing people to levitate from their beds. In most cases the problems will subside as the child matures or, indeed, is removed from the premises. The individual concerned is completely unaware that it is their emotional energy that is involved. It is unusual for poltergeistal activity to be of any duration. In some cases it lasts only for a few days, whereas in others it may last a number of months.

In this case it was obviously out of the question for Charlie to be removed from his home. The poor lad had suffered more than enough over the past three months. What I had to do was clear the atmosphere and make it impossible for a build-up of negative energy to be maintained within the room. It was also important to give Charlie the opportunity to express his anxieties so he could be free of the emotional turmoil that he had going on inside him.

Whilst we waited, I informed Delia that it was my intention to conduct a candle rite in order to cleanse the atmosphere of her home. I always carry the necessary candles, salt and white sheet in a special bag with me in my car. My only other requirement was a bowl of water, which Delia went to fetch from the kitchen whilst I recovered the necessary items from the car.

Charlie arrived home at 3.30 p.m. Delia introduced me to him and then he retreated upstairs to his room. Almost as soon as we heard his footsteps go up the stairs and enter his bedroom, which was directly over the room in which we were sitting, a strange scratching sound could be heard coming from above us. This was followed by a rapid knocking noise as though someone was drumming their feet against the floor.

I stood up. 'Would you take me up to Charlie's bedroom again?' I asked Delia.

Delia, Ray and I climbed the stairs once more, stopping directly outside Charlie's bedroom. An odd whirring noise seemed to be coming from within.

Delia opened the door for me. Charlie was sitting on a chair next to his bed looking petrified. 'It's happening again, Grandma!' he shouted. He leaped up and threw himself into his grandmother's arms.

The atmosphere in the room was putrid and extremely cold. When I walked in, it felt as though I had walked into a refrigerator. Although the window wasn't open, the curtains were fluttering against the windowpane. It appeared to be dark and to be getting darker. I asked Delia to take Charlie downstairs whilst Ray remained with me.

I sat down on the chair which Charlie had recently vacated and called upon Sam and my other guides and helpers to assist me. There was not a shadow of a doubt that Charlie's emotional state was the cause of the disruptions being experienced in the house. The moment that he had walked out of the room, the disturbances had diminished to an odd scrabbling sound.

Ray passed me my bag. I laid the white sheet upon a small table in the room. First I sprinkled it with a little water and then a small amount of salt. I then placed four white candles on the table in a row, with three green candles slightly in front of them. I lit the candles and prayed. First I prayed to God to wrap me and the other occupants of the house in the white light of protection and eternal love. Then I prayed to God and to the spirit universe to use their powers to disperse the disruptive energies that were plaguing this poor boy and this home. I threw salt to the four corners of the room, representing the four corners of the universe, in order to cleanse this boy and his home and keep them safe.

After a while the atmosphere gradually began to lighten. Now I could see sunshine outside the window. The oppressive silence that had pervaded the room began to be broken by sounds from the garden. I felt sure that my prayers had been answered and that the atmosphere had now been cleared.

As I collected my things together, I turned one last time to look around the room. One particular corner seemed far brighter than the others. As I looked across at it, I saw the spirit form of a young woman materialize. She was a serene-looking soul with long fair hair and blue eyes. She did nothing other than smile at me and nod in acknowledgement, but I heard Sam murmur, 'Rebecca thanks you for helping her son.'

Ray and I went back downstairs. I was happy to be able to tell Delia that the atmosphere in her home was now completely clear and that Charlie wouldn't be bothered any longer by the strange disturbances. His mother was close to him and wouldn't allow any more negative energies to build up around him. Although she had only recently passed to the spirit world, she would remain by her son's side, building up her own energies as she did so.

I also suggested to Delia that Charlie might benefit from speaking to a bereavement counsellor. That would definitely help him to release the anguish he had bottled up after the loss of his mother. Sometimes children find it difficult to express themselves properly to grandparents or teachers, regardless of how close they are to them, and find it easier to speak to a stranger who is trained to deal with children who have recently been bereaved.

Delia agreed. 'I had begun to think along those lines myself,' she told me, 'but I'd been waiting to see if Charlie would open up to me and talk things over.'

On my last trip to Hastings Delia turned up at the theatre with her husband Michael. After the show she told me that everything seemed fine at home. There had been no repetition of the awful disturbances that had gone on earlier. I was overjoyed to hear that Charlie was a lot happier too. Although he naturally missed his mother terribly, he seemed able to talk about her more openly now.

'And did you seek out a counsellor for him?' I asked Delia.

'Yes, I did,' she replied, 'and it's the best thing I could have done for him.'

CHAPTER NINE

An Unwanted Visitor

I was exhausted. I had been on the road from town to city and back to town again for eight consecutive days. Working without a break, whether filming or demonstrating in theatres, may look effortless to the onlooker, but it isn't. I don't think people realize the mental strain mediums undergo.

Ray and I were on our way to Eastbourne. Some days earlier I had taken a telephone call from a man who had introduced himself as Brian. He had told me that he and his wife Nancy had tickets to see me at the theatre in Eastbourne but that he would very much appreciate it if he could have a word with me after the show. I had told him that I always stay behind after demonstrations and that if he would like to, he and his wife were welcome to have a word with me then.

I had almost completed the signing session in the foyer of the theatre when a couple presented themselves in front of me. They were a pleasant-looking pair who were neatly turned out.

'Hi, Derek. I'm Brian and this is my wife Nancy.'

Brian was of medium height with premature balding, but he was a strong-looking man – a man a person could depend on. His wife Nancy was very slight of build and seemed to have a nervous air about her.

I stood up and shook their hands. 'If you would just wait for ten minutes or so whilst I complete these signings, I'll be with you,' I told them.

When the last person in the queue had disappeared through the door, I turned my attention to Brian and his wife. 'How can I help you?' I asked.

Brian shook his head. 'I don't know whether you *will* be able to help,' he told me. 'Nancy and I are at our wits' end. We just don't know what to do. We're in a nightmare predicament.'

Brian told me their story. Nancy, he said, had always been a marvellous wife and mother, but for too long she had held back a terrible secret from her past. As a child she had lived with her mother and father, her sister Susie and her brother Peter. Her childhood had not been a happy one, as the children had suffered the cruellest of abuse, both physical and mental, at the hands of their father. If their mother had interfered in any way then she, too, had received terrible beatings. The horror culminated in Nancy being raped by her father whilst only 12 years of age. She had tried to tell her mother, but had been so afraid of the consequences that in the end she had remained silent, in spite of the abuse continuing. She had left home as soon as she possibly could at the age of 16.

After that, she had not visited her parents' house at all. She had kept in sporadic contact with her brother and her sister, but felt let down and angry that her mother had not intervened in some way to prevent the abuse or taken the children away from their father alto-gether. She also felt angry that she had not been able to unburden herself about her father's sexual abuse.

Nancy then went on to tell me that she had been heartbroken to hear, some years later through her brother and sister, that her mother was suffering terminal cancer and did not have long to live. Her father, she learned, had passed away only a month or two earlier. She decided that she would visit her mum in hospital.

By the time Nancy arrived, her mother was heavily drugged for most of the time, but sometimes she would reminisce and recall the harsh times they had all suffered at Nancy's father's hands.

'Why on Earth didn't you go to the police about him?' Nancy asked her mother. 'You couldn't have loved him, surely?'

'I did and I didn't. He didn't touch Susie, you know. It was only you, because you looked so much like me,' her mother replied.

As Nancy related this story to me I realized that unfortunately this was a case where people have to undergo certain harsh experiences in their lifetime in order to achieve soul growth. In other words, they had agreed to these experiences before they had incarnated into their physical bodies.

I asked Nancy whether her father had taken drugs or been an alcoholic and his personality had changed after taking such substances.

Nancy exclaimed, 'Oh no! He was a pillar of society and respected by his peers outside the home. They didn't know that a monster lay within.'

She went on to tell me that her father had held a position of authority in his workplace and had earned a very good salary. He had provided a comfortable home and to everyone outside his family he was a very successful man.

Time was passing and I still had not reached the reason for Brian and Nancy's desire to see me.

'I don't see how I can help,' I told them. 'What has happened has nothing to do with the paranormal. I think you could achieve more by speaking to an experienced counsellor than a medium.'

'Oh no, you don't understand, Derek. We haven't finished yet!' Brian exclaimed.

Nancy proceeded to explain. 'It all began when Brian and I started doing rather well.' She told me that through hard work and endeavour, they had gradually built up a nice home and had been able to enjoy the better things in life. They had been able to afford all the material things they had ever wished for and enjoyed nice holidays a couple of times a year. But although she had everything she could possibly want, she had always had a fascination for her old home – the house where she had been brought up and where she had suffered so much at the hands of her father. 'I always felt that I would like a house exactly like that one,' she told me.

A couple of years later, whilst leafing through a magazine advertising houses for sale around the country, Nancy had been surprised to see a very familiar building up for sale: her old home. There it was, with its five bedrooms, outbuildings and three acres of land. Not only that, but Nancy noticed that planning permission had been granted to build yet another house on the land.

'I just wanted that house,' she told me. 'We were in a position to afford it and so I made initial enquiries. I thought that if we moved there, all my old demons would be laid to rest by making it into a happy home.'

Brian, who had been aware of what Nancy had experienced in her old home, only agreed to the purchase reluctantly. He was not so sure about the wisdom of Nancy's decision, but because he loved her and wanted only her happiness, he agreed to sell up and move home.

It was only when they actually moved that the full realization of the mistake they had made became abundantly clear. Nancy was not the only person for whom the old home held a fascination. Her father, who had passed away some years before, still remained within the building. He had not moved on at all. His spirit still roamed the rooms and landings of the old home and now he was making Nancy's life hell. Everywhere she went in her home she could feel him alongside her. When she went to bed at night an unseen hand would rip the bedclothes off her and roam over her body. Personal items would go missing and anything that Brian bought her would be damaged or smashed. Even if she was working in the kitchen on something special for Brian, she would find that the food would inexplicably burn and be inedible.

Although I was tired and just wanted to complete this leg of my theatre tour and go home, I agreed to delay my departure the following day and visit Brian and Nancy in order to establish whether I could be of any assistance to them in their predicament. I felt that it was likely I would be able to persuade Nancy's father to move on to his proper place in the spirit world and begin his progression towards true salvation in atoning for his sins towards his daughter whilst here on Earth.

* * *

The moment I walked through the door of Brian's and Nancy's home the following morning, I was aware of a dark and brooding presence. I picked up deep animosity directed towards Brian. I realized that Nancy's father was actually jealous of her husband. He did not want to share her with another man; he wanted her to himself. Even though he had passed on to the world of spirit, he remained in the lower realms, still driven by his physical urges and the same unreasoned sense of 'ownership' of his elder daughter.

'He's here, isn't he, Derek?' Nancy stated. 'I can feel him. I can feel him all around the place.'

I agreed that her father was indeed making his presence felt.

'What was his name?' I asked.

'George,' she replied. 'His name was George.'

I walked around the ground floor of the house. As I did so I was aware of the brooding presence of George watching my every move. He said nothing and nor did he show himself in spirit form, but he was there nonetheless.

I asked Sam to remain close by me. 'I'm here, Derek,' he reassured me. 'We will rid this home and this woman's life of this problem.'

I felt heartened to know that Sam was with me. I called upon my guardians and gatekeepers to also remain close by me. Then I called upon the spirits of George's family to come to collect their son and to help him atone for his wrong-doings whilst here in his physical life.

I asked Brian and Nancy to take me up to the bedroom that Nancy had occupied as a child, the place where she had suffered so much at the hands of her father.

'That's the only room we don't use at all,' Brian told me.

Nevertheless, that was where I wanted to go. I felt there was a need to cleanse the room spiritually, thereby ridding the home of the portal George used to enter the atmosphere of the building.

The three of us gathered in the room. It was chilly and the brooding energy I had felt on the ground floor of the house was more intense here.

In front of me the form of a man in spirit began to build. Surprisingly, he was unremarkable looking, but I could feel the intensity of his hatred towards me. He was determined that I would not remove him from the position where he could carry on demonstrating his warped emotions towards his daughter Nancy.

Brian, Nancy and I joined hands and prayed to the spirit world. I demanded that George be collected and moved on and away from Nancy's physical life. Long and hard I prayed to the higher spirit beings to assist in ridding this home of his presence.

I could see from the expression on George's face that a battle was taking place with him spiritually. He looked almost in pain, with staring eyes and gritted teeth. It was though he was holding on as hard as he could. Slowly, he began to lose the battle. The onslaught of so much positive spiritual energy was too much for him. With an agonized glance in Nancy's direction, his outline began to fade and then, after a few moments, disappeared completely.

'It is done,' I heard Sam tell me. 'He is gone. He will not return.'

I slowly released the tight grip I had held on Brian and Nancy's hands. I felt exhausted – I had expended so much physical and emotional energy.

I told Brian and Nancy that I had been promised that they would never be bothered again.

'Thank you, Derek,' they both said.

I told them that their thanks were not due to me, but to their own loved ones in the spirit world and to

George's – decent people who had lived their physical lives without blame and who had passed on to the higher side of life.

'This room seems so much brighter and lighter now,' Nancy remarked.

I explained to her that because it had now been cleansed by spiritual light and energy, she would never again be loath to walk through its door.

'I don't know, Derek,' she said. 'My father may be gone now, but the bad memories of that room still remain. I love this house and I know now that I will love living here, but whether I will use that room or not, I really don't know.'

'Well, if you won't,' said Brian, 'I'll have it as my hobbies room. I've been thinking about it for a while now. I'll be able to keep all my bits and pieces up here without fear of you clearing everything away!' He laughed.

I was happy to see the lightness and joy that now permeated the atmosphere of the house. As I wearily walked back to where Ray was waiting for me in the car, I was pleased that I had been able to help. I could now get on the road and travel back up north to my own safe haven.

CHAPTER TEN

The Old Hall Hotel

The Old Hall Hotel is set in the ancient spa town of Buxton, Derbyshire. Walking into it is, in parts, like taking a stroll back through time. The building itself dates back to the middle 1500s and even before then there was another dwelling on the site.

I was enchanted by the hotel the moment I walked through its doors. I had been driven to the location by the production team of Granada Breeze Television in order to record an investigation for the programme *Predictions with Derek Acorah*. I knew immediately the hotel was pointed out to me that I would enjoy investigating it.

We were welcomed by the manager of the hotel, who immediately arranged coffee for us in a lounge. As the production crew had not visited the location earlier, they took time to walk around and acquaint themselves with the areas in which they wished to film. I, meanwhile, sat back, relaxed and drank in the atmosphere. Even before opening myself up to the vibrations of the building I could feel that I was in a place with a lot of history, history that dated back many hundreds of years. The fabric of the building exuded a regal presence that told me that a person or persons of high standing had graced its portals. I could not wait to commence the investigation to discover more of the old hotel's past.

The production crew returned from their wanderings around the building. 'It's a beautiful old place, isn't it, Derek?' commented Rachel, the producer. 'Are you picking up anything at the moment?'

I told her that although I was not open at that particular time, as I was saving my energies for the filming, I knew that the place had a rich and chequered history.

'I'll say!' Rachel replied.

It was time to begin the investigation.

I walked through the room where we had been sitting towards the door. As I did so, the whole interior changed. It was like taking a step back in time. The empty room took on an air of days long gone. A group of men sat at ease in high-backed chairs. They were learned looking and some of them were smoking long-stemmed pipes. I heard the name 'Daniel' whispered.

I turned to Rachel to see whether she had noticed anything at all, but her eyes were firmly fixed on the door. She was chatting to the manageress as she walked.

'Does the name "Daniel" mean anything at all?' I asked.

'Oh yes,' the manageress replied. 'Daniel Defoe, the famous author, used to come here to write sometimes.'

'I *was* in learned company,' I thought to myself.

As I climbed the stairs to an upper floor I began to prepare myself by opening up my mind to the atmosphere of the hotel. I whispered my prayer of protection for myself and the crew around me. It is my rule to myself that I will never go anywhere without asking the higher side of life for protection of all concerned when undertaking a paranormal investigation. Anybody who has ever worked with me knows this. It may not always be spoken about, but nevertheless they are very well aware that this is my practice. Once again I must empha-size at this point that it is a very important procedure for anybody who is contemplating entering an allegedly 'haunted' location. To ignore the fact is foolish in the extreme. I have known occasions where people have chosen to dismiss a medium's advice regarding spiritual protection, only to be very sorry at the end of the day.

I arrived at a landing at the top of the stairs. I immediately became aware of the spirit form of a gentleman. He was dressed in garb dating back many, many years. It was similar to the dress of men I had seen in portraits painted around Elizabethan times. Next to him, with her hand lightly placed on his arm, stood a lady in similar dress. They both had the haughty demeanour of the nobility of the time. They proceeded towards me and the crew, melting into nothingness as they almost drew level with us.

I stopped briefly to absorb the atmosphere of the place. I had not realized how old it was when I had arrived, but upon entering the building and viewing the interior and especially now, after having seen a couple of the less worldly inhabitants, I knew that it dated back many hundreds of years.

I kept hearing the name 'George, George' echoing in my ears, though I did not receive any more information at that moment in time.

We continued walking down creaking corridors. Rachel and her assistant clung on to one another at every groan and squeak. 'And it's not even dark!' they laughed.

I described what I was seeing. There were impressions of life as it had been in the sixteenth century, with maids bustling about their business tending to the needs of their aristocratic employers. And although I could pick up no evidence of treachery, I certainly got the feeling of plans and intrigue. I received the definite impression of men meeting together and taking part in deep discussions, discussions that I could only describe as almost 'parliamentary' in content.

Time after time I would glimpse snatches of times long gone by. I knew of course that what I was seeing was not spirit people but what I would describe as 'photographs in time' – memories that are held in the atmosphere of an old building, absorbed into the brickwork forever.

The crew and I continued along the corridor until we reached the door of a room. It was dark and shiny and obviously very old. Rachel opened the latch and pushed it open. It was the door to a bedroom – and a luxurious bedroom at that. It contained a four-poster bed that was furnished with heavy tapestries and drapes. The window was comparatively small and leaded.

I walked into the room and stood in the centre. I remained quite still for some time. There was so much residual energy in the room – in fact in the whole of the building – that my senses were swimming with information.

As I walked around the sumptuous bedroom at the Old Hall Hotel, I noticed the spirit form of a lady building up next to one of the windows. I was shocked. The last person I had expected to see was Mary, Queen of Scots.

I had first come across the spirit of Mary some months previously at Tutbury Castle and during that first visit to Tutbury I had also been told that she would show herself again there. Some weeks later, when I returned to the castle to visit a medieval display there, Lesley Smith, the curator, had advised me that Mary's spirit had indeed appeared on the battlements.

I knew that Mary had travelled around extensively, mainly at the behest of Queen Elizabeth I. She had kept Mary on the move because she was afraid that her sympathizers would attempt to free her from imprisonment and encourage her to make a bid for the throne. Sightings of Mary's spirit have since been reported in numerous locations throughout Scotland and England. Although these may well be accurate, I knew her spirit body could only be in one place at any particular time. In spirit the same rule applies as in life: we can only be in one place at once.

When I had happened upon Mary at Tutbury she had seemed to be a sad and unhappy soul. This time she seemed lighter of spirit. Was it really her?

'It is indeed the lady Mary,' I heard Sam whisper to me.

I looked across to her. As I did so, she sat down on a small chair and took up some needlework. I could not see what it was that she was creating, but I did have the distinct impression that this was something she enjoyed doing and that she was very proud of the results.

She stood up once more and wandered across to look through the window, placing her hands against the small leaded panes. Then, as a mist is dispersed by sunlight, her spirit form began to disappear. The room, though, was filled with the essence of her being.

I felt great sadness for the lady. She had been kept and watched over for so long, only to eventually meet her untimely end at Fotheringhay in Northamptonshire. I turned to Rachel and wondered out loud why I would be seeing Mary here in Derbyshire.

'Oh, she was here, Derek,' Rachel told me. She walked over to the spot by the window so recently vacated by the spirit of Queen Mary and pointed to an inscription etched into the glass. 'She is said to have written this with a diamond ring: "Buxton, whose warm waters have made thy name famous, perchance I shall visit thee no more – Farewell."'

I have to say that I am not so sure that Mary wrote those words herself. If she did, then I am wrong, but I very much doubt it.

We carried on through the hotel, going from room to room. There was an abundance of spiritual and residual energy there.

After the investigation, the manageress informed us that Mary, Queen of Scots, had indeed been kept there under house arrest for almost 10 years under the guardianship of George Talbot, Earl of Shrewsbury, who was married to Bess of Hardwick, a great friend of Elizabeth I.

The Old Hall Hotel is a fascinating place indeed. It has a rich history and an atmosphere conducive to ghost hunting. Its haunted corridors should sate the appetite of anybody who wishes to spend some time listening for 'things that go bump in the night'. It is many years now since I visited the hotel, but although the interior may have changed in that time, the spirits most certainly never will.

Chapter Eleven

A Very Big Mistake

Some years ago, before I moved to the Southport area, whilst I was still living in Liverpool, I was jolted awake one morning by the sensation of somebody attempting to pull the bedclothes off me. I lifted my head off the pillow and looked around the room. As my befuddled mind cleared itself of sleep, I could see standing alongside the bed the dark outline of a man in spirit.

'Who are you?' I asked mentally. 'What d'you want?'

There was silence.

I sat up in bed and looked at him. He was still there, but although I prompted him many times to respond, he remained silent.

It was as his spirit outline was finally beginning to weaken and disperse that suddenly one word rang out: 'Bastard!'

I was shocked.

'Don't you know what awaits you?' demanded the disembodied voice in ringing tones. 'You'll be damned forever!'

I was bewildered. I swung my legs out of the bed and walked towards the window. I opened the curtains to see that it was getting light outside. A quick glance at my bedside clock told me that it was still quite early in the morning and well before the time I usually rose, but because I was now wide awake, I decided to take a shower and start my day. As I stood under the hot jets of the shower, I wondered what on Earth had prompted the events of a few minutes ago.

After breakfast I got into my car and drove into Liverpool city centre, where I had my office. I was booked throughout the day for readings.

I completed four readings in the morning before I broke off for a spot of lunch. When I returned to the building, my two o'clock appointment was already in the waiting room. I noticed that it was a man and woman who were sitting together, although I knew that my appointment was with somebody who had made a phone booking under the name of 'Eileen'.

At two o'clock on the dot I opened my office door and invited Eileen into the room. 'D'you mind if my husband Jack comes in with me?' she asked. I told her that I had no objection whatsoever, just as long as she did not mind him hearing the content of her sitting. 'Well, the reason I've come to see you concerns both of us,' she replied.

I showed Eileen and her husband into the room and asked them to sit in the chairs on the other side of my desk. The moment they sat down Jack told me, 'We've been to hell and back, Derek! We daren't say anything to anybody in case they think we're cranks, but we're not. We're truly experiencing what we're about to tell you.'

Jack told me their story. Nothing seemed to be going right in their lives. Strange and ridiculous things were happening. He gave a 'for instance'. They had run out of milk and Jack had decided that he would cycle to the small shop close by for some more. Eileen had noticed that he had been gone for rather a long time and so had gone to their gate to see whether she could see him coming down the road. What she saw startled her. Jack had almost reached the house, but he was pushing his bike, its wheels were wobbly and he had torn and bloodied knees to his trousers and horrible scrapes on his hands. He looked as though he had been involved in an accident.

Jack explained to Eileen that he had been pedalling along to the shop, which was only at the end of their road, when suddenly, for no reason whatsoever, the bike had collapsed underneath him. He said that he felt almost as though he had been pushed and, to make matters worse, this had happened just as a car was overtaking him.

'I was damned lucky not to have gone under its wheels,' Jack informed me.

That was just one incident. There had been others where Jack had been in a seemingly safe situation that had turned into something very dangerous indeed.

'It's almost as though something's following him all the time, intent on doing him harm,' Eileen told me. 'I'm very frightened and whatever it is doesn't leave me alone either. The other day when I was hanging out some washing I was prodded very hard in my back. It was though someone had picked up a stick and poked it right into my ribs. Would you agree to come to our home to see whether you can find out what's causing the problem?'

I have experienced times when people have fallen victim to a very vivid imagination and have related fantastic stories to me, only for me to discover that what they were thinking of as paranormal interference was in fact due to entirely ordinary, physical and logical events. After the first couple of times when I involved myself in a wild goose chase, I realized that I should first check with Sam to ensure that there was indeed a spiritual explanation for what was going on. He would advise me. Now I could tell that Jack and Eileen were entirely sincere, and Sam was with me on this. 'You can help the people,' he murmured.

I told Jack and Eileen that I would call at their home when I had completed my day's work in the office. They gave me their address and told me that they would be waiting for me.

I arrived at the house around 5 p.m. Jack met me at the door and showed me into the kitchen.

'It was out there that I was prodded when I was hanging out the washing,' said Eileen, pointing to a gravelled area in the back garden.

As I sat in the kitchen I noticed that there were youngsters' clothes folded over the back of one of the kitchen chairs. 'You have sons?' I asked.

'Yes,' said Jack. He told me that they had two boys – Lee, who was aged 15, and Barry, now 13. As he finished speaking, the front door opened and closed and footsteps were heard coming along the hallway. The kitchen door opened and the two boys themselves walked in. They had just been to football practice. Eileen introduced me to them and we had a chat about football for a few moments.

'Mr Acorah's not here to hear you two yammering on about your games,' Eileen told them eventually. She explained that I had called at the house to see whether I could help with what had been going on recently.

'You're a ghost hunter then?' Lee asked, his eyes gleaming with interest.

I noticed that Barry was more reluctant to discuss this and left the room.

I explained to Lee that I was not in fact a 'ghost hunter' but a medium and, as such, I tried to help when people were being bothered by incidents that were suspected of having a less than worldly cause.

'So the paranormal interests you a lot?' I asked him.

'Oh yeah,' he replied.

I began to have feelings of unease.

Lee's next question made me sit up even straighter. 'So, do you find it easy to evoke the good and bad spirits?' he asked.

I asked him why he would ask me a question like that and in reply I heard a snigger from the doorway. Barry had returned.

'Lee thinks he's a big ghost hunter 'cos he plays the ouija board and gets messages,' he said.

The whole picture was becoming abundantly clear to me now.

I asked whether I could speak to Jack and Eileen alone. We left Lee and Barry in the kitchen making some tea and toast and retired to the sitting room at the front of the house.

'Are your sons close as brothers?' I asked Eileen.

She replied that they were extremely close and were almost inseparable away from school, even though there were two years between them.

I asked whether she could remember who had been the first person in the family to notice anything untoward. 'Oh, it was Lee,' she replied. 'He came downstairs once to say that there were strange noises in his bedroom.'

171

Apparently it had not been long before Barry had been complaining of the same thing. They had both, at different times, told Eileen that the drains must need cleaning because of the terrible smell upstairs. She had also noticed that on occasion the boys' bedroom furniture seemed to have moved from where it should be – she was forever putting things back to rights.

As we had been speaking I had noticed that the atmosphere in the room had begun to smell rather stale. I was also aware that the energies were beginning to feel a little negative. 'Were you aware that your sons conducted ouija board sessions?' I asked Jack and Eileen.

They looked at one another. 'We're not sure what a ouija board is,' Jack told me.

I explained to them that ouija boards had been popular as a parlour game since Victorian times. A board or table top is used with the letters of the alphabet arranged in a circle, together with the words 'yes' and 'no' and the numbers one to ten. An upturned glass is placed in the middle of the circle. The players place their index fingers upon the bottom of the tumbler and a spokesperson is designated to ask the spirit world to pass on messages by directing the tumbler to individual letters, thus spelling out messages. Simple questions can be asked and the theory is that the glass will be guided to the words 'yes' and 'no'.

I explained that I had come across incidents before when people, through idle curiosity, had created a ouija board, not knowing that they could inadvertently evoke spirits from the lower orders of the spirit realms who were bent on creating mischief.

'Oh dear,' said Eileen. 'D'you think that's what's behind the problems we're having?'

I told her that I most certainly did think so.

Suddenly we heard a noise coming from upstairs. There was the sound of glass breaking and then the loud bang of a door slamming shut, followed by the noise of feet scurrying down the stairs. The door to the room in which we were sitting was flung open and Barry flew into the room.

'Quick, Derek! You've got to come and help! Lee's acting really funny and I'm scared!' he shouted.

Jack, Eileen and I rushed up the stairs. Jack flung open the door of Lee's bedroom. Lee was sitting on the edge of the bed with his eyes closed. In front of him was a table set up for a ouija session. The smashed remains of a tumbler lay on the floor to the side of the small table. The expression on Lee's face was blank. His features were set and stern. He looked much older than his years.

I summoned protection for everyone from my guides and helpers and the doorkeepers of all in the home. I was aware of Sam standing very close by me, filling me with the strength of his presence.

Lee opened his eyes, but they were lifeless and dead and much darker in colour than his natural blue. Eileen gasped as he began to speak. I recognized immediately the voice I had heard that morning – the voice that had disturbed my sleep so many hours earlier in the day.

The words uttered from Lee's mouth were nothing less than vile. 'Bastard!' came the scream time and time again, in a voice much deeper than that of a 15-year-old lad.

I walked over to him. As I approached him, he stood up suddenly. Feeling the strength of my guides and protectors around me, I placed my hands on his shoulders. I closed my own eyes and prayed hard that this spirit would be sent back to the lower realms, to the world from which he had come.

'Pray for peace and light!' I shouted to Jack and Eileen. I heard them behind me intoning the only prayer with which they were familiar, the Lord's Prayer.

Time and again we prayed, over and over. Slowly I felt Lee begin to relax. His features took on those of a 15-year-old boy once more. The negative energy within him drained and gradually disappeared. He flopped on to the bed, sweating in fear.

'I'm sorry, Mum and Dad,' he said quietly. 'I thought that it would be fun to have a ouija session with our Barry while Derek was here.'

At that point we heard the door creak open behind us. The embarrassed face of Barry appeared. 'I'm sorry too,' he said sheepishly.

I explained to Jack, Eileen and their two boys how dangerous it was to attempt to evoke the spirit world in the manner in which they had done it. I stressed that I did not like the use of ouija boards, and if such things were to be used at all, it should only be done in the presence of an experienced medium. I told the two boys that this time they had got off lightly. Although there had been several minor disruptions, their mother had been frightened and upset, and there had also been occasions when their father could quite easily have been badly hurt. They were also extremely lucky that the spirit they had evoked had not been one of any particular strength. It could well have turned out to be a completely different and more horrible story.

Both boys were thoroughly chastened. They promised that they would never attempt anything like that again and I believe that they kept their word.

The next time Eileen visited me at my office for a reading she was able to report that all was peaceful in their house once more. There had been no repeat of the inexplicable incidents and Lee and Barry appeared to be happier and more at ease now.

CHAPTER TWELVE

Kensal Green Cemetery

When I first visited Kensal Green cemetery, I was a complete stranger to it. In fact I am ashamed to say that I had never heard of England's oldest surviving commercial cemetery before. I had not actually given any thought to the provenance of cemeteries in general, assuming that they were usually fairly small plots attached to churches. I was amazed, therefore, upon arriving at the cemetery to see the size of the place and to witness the number of graves and memorials of wondrous and intricate design.

I had been invited to Kensal Green by the makers of a programme featuring Alan Carr, one of the UK's foremost comedians. Gwen had kindly agreed to accompany me and I was glad that she did, as a three-hour train journey twice in one day is more than a little boring when you have to undertake it on your own.

It was with some trepidation that I stepped into the car that collected me from Euston station and was to carry me to the location for the filming. As we entered the heavy London traffic, I had no idea where we were heading. I was extremely surprised, therefore, to find that half an hour later we were entering the gates of a cemetery hard on the heels of a convoy of cars making for the crematorium in the grounds.

'This can't be right,' I commented to the driver. 'We're in the middle of somebody's funeral here!'

'This is the address I've been given,' he replied.

With that I took out my mobile phone and made a call to the producer of the production company.

'No, you've gone to the wrong part,' he informed me. 'You should have gone to the chapel. Go back to the gate and I'll meet you there. You can then follow me to the right place.'

I heaved a sigh of relief. I gave the driver instructions to retrace his steps and we duly met the producer at the west gate and followed him to the correct location.

* * *

Upon arriving, I was rather bemused to have my hand shaken by a tall chap dressed up as the Grim Reaper, complete with scythe. Alan Carr introduced himself. 'So pleased you could make it, Derek,' he told me.

After a quick run through the script, filming began. I was a little unnerved at the writing and wondered at the wisdom of its content, but I had signed on the dotted line and was therefore at the mercy of the production company. I hoped that people would appreciate the programme's light-hearted take on what I was doing. I am more than sure that the subjects of the sketches would have been howling with laughter.

As many people know, I am absolutely hopeless with scripts. I cannot remember words and so had to be provided with what are commonly known in the business as 'dummy boards'. Even then I managed to mess things up on more than one occasion, sometimes requiring as many as four or five takes. Filming progressed, though, and I got quite into the swing of things, while trying unsuccessfully to ignore Alan's hilarious innuendo and humour.

It was during a break when I was not required in the filming that I decided to wander with Gwen around the cemetery. It was so cold that it was impossible to stand still.

I was amazed at the number of headstones and family mausoleums within the cemetery's walls. There were row after row of graves, some dating back to the first half of the nineteenth century. We were absolutely amazed. It was sad to see the family graves where some five or six children, all only days, weeks or months old, had been buried. These dated back to the days when infant mortality was common. Women often have endured multiple pregnancies, only to lose their children in very early infancy. There were also the graves of women buried with their newborns, obviously having succumbed to infection and complications when giving birth.

We looked with interest at the graves of the great and the good of Victorian high society. Curiously, shoulder to shoulder with these huge Victorian architectural edifices were the ordinary gravestones common today: black granite or white marble with gold or black lettering, the odd urn containing fresh flowers indicating that the plot was often visited, proof that the grave's occupant was still very much loved and missed. There were also memorials to family members with notices that their remains were buried elsewhere in the country – something I did not know could happen. It was fascinating but somehow macabre to be wandering around peering curiously at these strangers' final resting-places.

We had wandered some few hundred yards when we decided to turn back. I was not sure how soon I could be required again for the filming and anyway darkness was falling rapidly. I did not want to get myself into the position of being lost in the middle of a strange cemetery with a production crew searching for me amongst the headstones. As we wandered slowly along the path-ways, it became too dark to read the lettering on the headstones, but we marvelled at the outlines of the huge memorials and tombs against the London skyline.

'It looks as though somebody's come looking for us,' Gwen commented as we continued along the pathway to the chapel.

Coming towards us was the vague outline of a man. Suddenly he disappeared.

'Where on Earth did he go?' Gwen asked after a moment or two. 'I only turned around for a moment and then he was gone!'

I did not like to tell her that after all this time she had probably experienced her first ghost sighting.

We carried on walking. As we reached the chapel I decided to turn around and take a few moments to see whether I could catch a further glimpse of the figure we had seen on the footpath.

I had gone no more than 50 yards or so when a few feet in front of me, standing next to a large monument, I spied another man in spirit. He wasn't solid, but quite ephemeral and vapour-like in appearance. I could vaguely make out the outline of the monument through his spirit body. I was surprised at his presence, because it is unusual for spirit people to return to the place where their earthly remains lie. They are far more likely to visit places they have enjoyed than the place where their physical bones lie rotting.

I asked Sam, 'Can I communicate with this soul?'

I heard a murmur of assent and the information that I was in the company of Andrew. I knew without a shadow of doubt that the name 'Florence' was impor-tant to him. I had an impression of children, but this feeling was accompanied by a great deal of sadness.

'Why are you here?' I asked softly.

Andrew looked sadly to his left. Following his gaze, in the dim light I could make out the outline of an ornate casket-shaped gravestone. It was embellished by small tablets of stone. I moved nearer and used the flame from my cigarette lighter to illuminate the writing.

What I saw saddened me. Each small tablet contained a name. Below each name was a date of birth and a date of passing to the world of spirit. The passing dates were almost identical. I moved the light up to show the name on the main grave. It was 'Florence'. She had passed at the same time as the children.

I walked the few paces back towards the spirit man. 'He feels he is to blame,' Sam told me. 'He was out working when his home caught fire and his family perished. Some were rescued from the flames, but not in time to save them. They all came over to the heavenly side within a day or two of one another.'

'But why isn't he with them?' I asked.

Sam explained to me that Andrew didn't feel that he had the right to join his family in their place in the spirit world. Over the years since his own passing he had robbed himself of his rightful place in heaven.

I decided to speak to Andrew. I explained that what had happened was not his fault and told him that he should join his family and enjoy his time with them. Until he did so, I knew that he would not achieve fulfilment and the right to incarnate into another earthly life. In other words, he was halting the progress of his own soul growth. He needed to rid himself of the blame he felt so strongly.

As I finished speaking, I saw a bright light begin to grow around his shoulders. I felt the warmth of angelic love surround him. Gradually his spirit outline evaporated. I knew that he was on his way to his rightful place in the heavenly state at long last.

I turned and walked back to the chapel.

'Where've you been?' demanded Gwen. 'People have been waiting for you.'

With filming completed, it was time to return to the cars waiting for us outside the cemetery gates. As Gwen and I trudged along the pathways between the gravestones, accompanied by Alan, I felt happy that I had been able to help Andrew in his plight.

I explained to Gwen why I had been delayed. 'Poor soul. How awful for him. I'm pleased you were able to help,' she said.

We reached the gates. Sure enough, the cars were waiting for us. There was just one problem – the gates were locked! A huge padlock was holding the massive wrought-iron affairs tightly closed and there was no hope of pulling them apart.

'Oh Gawd!' Alan groaned. 'That's all we need! Alan Carr and Derek Acorah locked in a graveyard! That'd make a fun headline in the "Out and About" section of *Heat* magazine!'

The vehicle drivers thought it an utterly hilarious situation and laughed helplessly at our predicament. Fortunately someone was able to locate a key and after about half an hour we were released and Gwen and I were on our way back to Euston station.

As the train was pulling out of the station Gwen commented, 'Well, I don't know whether you're cut out for comedy, Derek, but at least today must have been meant. If you hadn't have come down here, you wouldn't have been able to help that poor chap.'

She was right. Once again, some things are meant to be!

I found my visit to Kensal Green cemetery so fascinating that Gwen looked up what my good friend Richard Jones had to say about it on his 'London Walking Tours' website. It reads as follows:

'All Souls Cemetery, Kensal Green, was founded in 1832 under the auspices of the Cemetery Company and was the first of the great commercial cemeteries to be in London. Today it is the oldest surviving English cemetery to remain in ownership. Charles Dickens chose it as the resting-place for his beloved sister Mary Hogarth and many of his literary acquaintances are buried at Kensal. Indeed, so many of the 19th century's great and good are buried here that to walk amongst its seemingly endless lines of gravestones and memorials is like walking through a *Who's Who* of 19th century society. Since many of the memorials were erected and composed whilst the ultimate occupants of the graves were still alive and stand as a timeless illustration of how important some of those buried here were considered in their lifetimes – or more to the point, how important those occupants considered themselves. It is a fascinating, though slightly chilling, experience to see the graves of so many people whose names dominated Victorian society.'

Richard goes on to say:

'Mary Hogarth (1820–1837) was the beloved sister-in-law of Charles Dickens. She died on 7th May 1837 and

Dickens was utterly bereft at her loss. At the time he was working on *Pickwick Papers* and *Oliver Twist* and he was unable to complete the next instalment of both. Rumours began to circulate that the talented young writer Boz (the name under which Dickens was writing) had gone insane, or even that he had committed suicide …

Dickens took immediate charge of the funeral arrangements for Mary and it was he who paid for her grave at Kensal Green Cemetery, and it was he who composed the epitaph that, although now somewhat weathered, can still be discerned on her tombstone – "Young, beautiful and good. God in His mercy numbered her amongst the angels at the early age of seventeen."'

If you wish to read more of what Richard has to say about Kensal Green cemetery, please visit his website at www.walksoflondon.co.uk.

CHAPTER THIRTEEN

Spanish Surprise

I have always loved Spain – the country, its people and its culture – so much so that a few years ago Gwen and I made the decision to buy a house there. Although this took some time to achieve, we are now the proud owners of a home in a part of the countryside not too far from the Crevillient Mountains on the Costa Blanca. Unlike many people (and there are upwards of a million British people now living in that part of Spain), we did not want to live too close to the beaches and the holiday-makers. We made the decision to buy something inland so that we could experience Spanish life as it really is and not the Spain that is packaged and sold to the holiday-maker. Even so, we have found that it is not too much of a culture shock, because the ever-encroaching building work has ensured that there are British communities throughout the area, which of course include the Great British supermarket.

It was whilst I was visiting one of these small retail outlets that I happened to bump into a man I had come to recognize as a frequent visitor to the shop. We had seen each other when we called in for our daily British newspapers, although we had not, up to that point, spoken to one another.

That morning, however, he approached me and introduced himself. 'Hello, my name's Bob,' he said. 'I've seen you coming in here a lot and I was wondering whether I could ask you, are you Derek Acorah off the telly?'

I admitted that I was.

'I *thought* it was you!' he exclaimed. 'I was telling my wife Maura that I was sure Derek Acorah was living around here because I'd seen you so often getting your newspapers.'

Bob went on to tell me that he and his wife had been living in Spain permanently for three years now and loved it. He said that they had no intention ever of returning to their roots in England. 'Why should we?

We have everything here – sun, sea, sand *and* English television!'

He told me that they loved to watch the LivingTV programmes 'about ghosts' and had seen me on numerous occasions when I had appeared on *Most Haunted*, *Antiques Ghost Show* and *Derek Acorah's Ghost Towns.*

'Why don't you ever do any ghost hunting over here?' he said. 'There are lots of places. Spain's very haunted.'

I explained that when I came to this part of Spain it was always as a holiday break or when I had time to myself and the weather was bad in England.

'You should move over here permanently,' Bob told me. 'You wouldn't have to worry about the weather then.'

With that we went our separate ways. 'I'll tell Maura I've met you,' he said as he disappeared into his car.

Over the duration of my stays in Spain I met Bob on numerous occasions, usually whilst collecting the daily newspapers and sometimes around and about the small town. Sometimes Maura was with him and she also used to say hello and chat. It was during one of my conversations with them that they told me about a friend who was experiencing some problems in his home. There was no explanation for what was going on and the problem had started quite suddenly. Bob and Maura asked me whether I could help.

Two days later saw me meeting Bob and Maura in the town centre. I was to follow them to their friend's home as, they explained, I would never find it on my own because it was tucked away in the countryside amongst the orange and lemon groves so prevalent in the area.

I was surprised when after driving down many dusty and winding roads we arrived at a small *finca*, a Spanish farm. The small farmhouse was surrounded by fields of orange and lemon trees, with fields of artichokes stretching into the distance. Quite close to the house and outbuildings stood the remains of a much larger and apparently much grander house. To one side, about 100 yards away, were two or three newly built houses. It was obvious to me that Bob and Maura's friend had sold a plot of his land to a building company, something which is quite common in the rural areas of this part of Spain. Indeed, I lived in a similar situation myself.

As we got out of our vehicles, a swarthy-looking man of middle age came out of the *finca*. He was smiling broadly. As Bob introduced Manolo to me, I was horrified to note that he only spoke very broken English. My grasp of the Spanish language was equally bad, but Bob assured me that he would act as interpreter – he spoke fluent Spanish now.

With Bob's assistance, Manolo told me his tale. He and his family had farmed the area for many generations. Originally they had occupied the large house. When his father, Manuel, had married, his grandfather, Joaquin, had arranged for the smaller farmhouse to be built so that his son could bring up his family independently from his parents. Manolo had been born and brought up in the smaller house.

As the years had passed, money had become short. When Joaquin had passed away, Manuel had stayed in the small *finca*. As there had been no money for the upkeep of the large house, it had been allowed to deteriorate and was now barely more than a few walls with a dilapidated roof. The only portion of the building which remained solid and in good repair was the section at the end of the house, one floor in height, which formed the stables or cowsheds.

I gazed at the building, thinking to myself how sad it was that such an obviously beautiful building had been left to fall into such a state of disrepair. With its fine windows and wrought-iron balconies, it must have been very impressive indeed once upon a time.

What was bothering Manolo was the fact that he and his wife Noemi had begun to notice disruption within their home. Items would go missing inexplicably, strange loud bumps had been heard on the upper floor, pictures had slipped from their hangings and there seemed to be a general air of disruption about the place. Manolo had never experienced this before and he had lived in the house all his life. Neither he nor his wife could understand it. Their four children, who had been brought up in the house, had now all left home, so they knew that nobody else could be responsible for the strange occurrences. It was getting to the stage where Noemi dreaded being left on her own in the house and would accompany Manolo whenever he had to go out. Life was becoming more than a little uncomfortable for them.

I asked whether I could go into the house to take a look around. Bob explained to Manolo that I would like to do this to get a 'feel' of the place – to see whether I could pick up anything psychically from the interior of his house. Manolo gladly agreed and led me to the door.

It was a relief to get out of the searing sun and into the shade. Noemi was sitting at the kitchen table preparing vegetables for a meal. She nodded to me politely as I passed through the room. I was startled to see that sitting in a chair next to an open fireplace was a spirit man. He was small and rotund and was smoking a long pipe. Although he was seated I could make out that he wore clothes similar to those of many of the old farmers I saw daily around the area. He didn't look at all pleased that I was there and totally ignored me.

I opened myself up further to the vibrations and asked Sam who the old man was.

'This is Manuel, Manolo's father,' he replied.

I carried on through the room and followed Manolo up the staircase to the upper floor. There were three bedrooms, each furnished in heavy old Spanish-style furniture with ewers and basins placed on ornate washstands. Each room had pictures on the wall, but they were so old and in need of cleaning that it was difficult for me to discern what they depicted. I could sense psychically that spiritual activity had been prevalent in all three rooms, though at that time there was no spirit presence. I got the distinct impression that the spirit person who had been walking around these rooms and making his presence felt was the very spirit man who was at that moment sitting in the kitchen downstairs.

After looking around, Manolo and I went back downstairs. I asked whether it would be possible to visit the old building adjacent to the farmhouse. Manolo indicated that it was not safe to go inside, but I was certainly welcome to look around the perimeter.

We braved the heat once more and walked the short distance to the derelict old building. Once again I could sense spirit activity. This wasn't due to the man who had been sitting in the kitchen, but to someone else. I slowly went around the building, clambering over great squares of sandstone to reach a small clear area which was as close to the house as I dared go, given its dilapidated state.

As I stood there I became aware of another spirit man. He was only some five foot four or five in height and was much slimmer than the spirit presence in the kitchen. He didn't appear to be particularly happy either, though – in fact he seemed very angry indeed. He was chattering away at me in Spanish and gesticulating with his arms.

I turned and looked over my shoulder at the area he was indicating and saw in the distance the newly built homes.

'What's he saying?' I asked Sam desperately. I had managed to pick up the odd word, but even the man's dialect seemed different from the Spanish I was used to hearing.

Sam explained to me that the spirit man in front of me was Manolo's grandfather, Joaquin. He was upset that some of the land he had tended so lovingly had been sold to a developer and used to build new homes and that 'foreigners' were living in them. It was he who had been visiting Manolo and Noemi's house, making the noises and causing the disruption in an effort to bring to their attention the fact that he was angry that they had sold some of what he still considered to be his land.

The spirit man had now come quite close to me and I could feel that he resented my very presence in the ruins of his old home. Close to me, a sandstone block suddenly shifted, and I leaped away to prevent it from rolling onto my foot. I knew that I had to get out of the immediate area rapidly, otherwise who knows what could have happened. Quickly, I scrambled across the broken wood and stones and back onto the dirt track which separated the two homes.

I told Bob what the spirit man had said and he, in turn, relayed the information to Manolo, whose eyes grew round with shock. He explained that the land had been sold to raise money so that his home could be repaired. Its roof had been leaking and the drainage system had required attention. Manolo didn't make much money as a farmer and had realized that the only way he could raise enough to carry out the repairs was to sell a small plot of land.

I asked Sam what could be done to alleviate the situation.

'We're already working on that problem,' he told me. He explained that Manuel, Manolo's father, was very unhappy about Joaquin's actions. He wanted Manolo and Noemi to live in peace. Did it matter that they had sold a small plot of land to make their lives a little more comfortable? Did it matter that the houses had been sold to people who weren't Spanish? We all live in this world and prejudices should be relinquished.

Bob, Manolo and I walked back to the small *finca*. As we went, with Bob's help, I explained the whole situation to Manolo. I told him that the spirit world was stepping in to calm Joaquin down and to help him come to terms with the changes in this physical world since the days when he was a young man. I asked him to look forward with optimism to a day not very long away when all would be peace and harmony once more.

As I got back into my car, I noted that the first spirit man, whom I now knew to be Manuel, was sitting next to the front door of the *finca*. He was still smoking, but I noticed that his face looked a little less dour – in fact I could almost swear that he was showing the glimmer of a smile.

A few days later I had to go back to England and it was some eight weeks before I returned once more to Spain and bumped into Bob in the local shop.

'Oh, you're back then, Derek! Good to see you,' he said.

He went on to tell me that following my visit to Manolo's home everything had begun to calm down. Within a couple of weeks Manolo and Noemi had noticed that the atmosphere felt much lighter and happier. There had been no more noises and Noemi was now happy to stay at home on her own once more.

There was only one thing that they couldn't explain and that was the fact that there seemed to be the smell of pipe smoke around the place, even though neither of them smoked.

I smiled to myself. Although Joaquin had decided to leave his grandson in peace, old Manuel was still around happily puffing away in his son's kitchen.

CHAPTER FOURTEEN

Locke's Distillery

During the summer of 2007 I was contacted by Bernadette Quinn, who managed Locke's Distillery in Kilbeggan, Co. Westmeath. Locke's, which dates back to 1757, is thought to be the oldest licensed pot still whiskey distillery in the world and produces some of the most sought-after Irish whiskey around today.

Bernadette had noticed that I would be in Ireland during the month of October, which coincided with a dinner planned for the people who had helped renovate the old distillery, and she wondered whether I would be prepared to conduct an investigation at the old building and attend the dinner later in the evening. I was more than happy to accept the invitation.

* * *

I flew into Dublin airport the evening before the investigation, together with Gwen, and the following morning I spent some time conducting interviews before travelling towards the small town of Tullamore, where we would be staying the night. This was only ten minutes' drive away from the distillery. Although the media interviews had been arranged in order to promote my tour of Ireland, I was so excited by the visit to Locke's that I couldn't prevent myself from telling people how much I was looking forward to it.

As we drove west from Dublin, I didn't know what to expect. I had never visited anywhere that produced spirits of the liquid variety before. As we approached the distillery, I was amazed to see how quaint it looked. It was easily identifiable by the large green 'Locke's Distillery' sign emblazoned on the side of the building, but it wasn't nearly as industrial as I had expected. The large white building was situated on the banks of the river Brusna, whose fast-flowing waters lapped green-lawned banks. It was an idyllic setting.

Travelling into the town of Kilbeggan, it was as though I had taken a step back in time. No huge supermarkets and none of the usual 'town shops' besmirched the high street winding through the small town.

I drove into the car park, parked up my hire vehicle and walked back across the parking area towards the office. As I walked, I could smell whiskey in the air.

I was welcomed into the office by Bernadette, who introduced me to Brian, her husband, who was to accompany us around the distillery during my investigation. He told me that the dinner that evening was being held in recognition of the hard work that had been undertaken by the local people who had helped restore the old distillery building. The work had commenced in 1982, some 25 years after the distillery had finally closed. I was amazed to realize that what I was about to enter was in fact a museum, albeit a working museum that still produced what seemed to me an enormous quantity of the renowned whiskey.

The moment I walked through from the office into the distillery itself, I was struck by the feeling of warmth and happiness emanating from the buildings. Wherever we went, I could pick up the fact that the employees, although toiling hard, were well treated and enjoyed their work. They looked upon their employers with reverence and were well looked after in return.

I walked through an open-ended building into a courtyard, past what appeared to my uneducated eye to be huge metal stills, and began my investigation proper.

Up the stairs we went, passing vast millstones along the way. All the time the atmosphere of industry and toil was evident, but it was nothing other than residual energy from the fabric of the building. It was as I entered a long gallery now containing large photographs of the distillery in former times that I encountered the first spirit presence. It was a lady. I was surprised to note that although obviously a person of some standing in the community, she was dressed in far more modern attire than I would have expected, complete with a small string of pearls at her neck.

I asked Sam to tell me who she was.

'This is Florence,' he told me, 'and she comes back here frequently.'

'Flo! Flo!' I said out loud.

I could pick up the affection for the old distillery that emanated from her, but also a sense of regret.

'Things could have been done differently. I had more to offer,' I heard a woman's voice tell me.

I was not at all sure what she was referring to and Bernadette and Brian didn't add anything to clear the matter up for me.

I tried hard to communicate with the spirit lady once more, but she was fading and receding back into the atmosphere and taking the tinges of regret with her. I was left with the feeling, however, that Flo was more than happy that her family name lived on and continued to be used. The only conclusion I could draw from that was that she had been a member of the Locke family, the founders of the old distillery.

'I need to go up those steps,' I said to Bernadette, pointing towards a short dogleg of stairs behind a rope barrier.

'Go ahead, Derek,' I was told.

I leaped up the steps and immediately came face to face with a gentleman from the spirit world – and he *was* a gentleman.

'This is John Edward,' Sam told me softly.

'I'm John,' the spirit man confirmed immediately, 'and I owned this place. It was mine!'

John was exceedingly proud of the distillery. He stood with his legs firmly planted on the floor and his thumbs hooked under his coat lapels, leaving me in no doubt as to his pride of ownership.

'We worked hard, all of us,' he told me, 'and I gave a good day's pay for a good day's work!'

I was aware that John was a regular visitor to his old stamping ground and I left him to continue his enjoyment of the old distillery. By the time I was walking out of the room he had turned and was looking out of the window, satisfaction emanating from his spirit body, owner of all he surveyed.

Down the stairs I went and out onto a small veranda. I looked to my left and saw the old waterwheel. I wondered whether it was still in use. I had no idea about the workings of a distillery, but imagined the wheel turning industriously against the strong current of the river below.

I went back inside the building. The energies were strong. I was not surprised to see yet another spirit man building up rapidly in front of me.

'Matthew! Matt! Mathias!'

I strained to hear the voice I was picking up clairaudiently. In contrast with John's proud bearing, this man was demonstrating an anger linked with a terrible sadness. I wondered whatever was making him manifest in this way. I realized he came from an earlier era than that of John Edward and, although I was not being told by either Sam or the spirit man himself, I wondered whether they were related in any way.

Then Sam cleared the picture for me. He told me that Mathias had had a son known as John who had become embroiled in political dealings and been executed because of his beliefs. John's spirit was now happy to remain in the distillery, as he had known peace and security there, but Mathias was very unhappy that he was not allowing himself to move forward into the spirit world proper and he came back frequently in order to encourage him to put behind him what had happened to him during his physical life on Earth. It was very sad and emotional – a father demonstrating his love for his son and wanting him to put the cares of his earthly life behind him so that he could move forward with his loved ones in spirit. No wonder Mathias was angry and upset.

I continued walking through the distillery, moving through the cooperage, where the barrels were repaired, and outside to an enormous hanger. I almost expected to see an aeroplane in the building, but discovered that it was a warehouse housing an enormous quantity of barrels of the distillery's delicious liquor.

Every area I visited was redolent with the industry of times gone by. Although this was still a working distillery, I knew that now there were nothing like the numbers of people who had once been employed there.

I was happy that my visit to Locke's Distillery had shown me that there was not a single spirit individual there who had anything negative about them and the whole atmosphere of the place was very positive. In their physical lives the employees had all been very good and well-intentioned people who had worked industriously towards a common aim, and when a person thinks well of another person, that love goes out into the ether and always remains in the fabric of a building, just as evil does.

I was happy to be able to inform Bernadette and Brian that the energies in the distillery were good and would continue to be so. I had picked up the disappointment and unhappiness of Mathias, but that was unrelated to the distillery itself. There was a certain sense of shock there that I felt had come about regarding a sudden stop, a cessation – that was all. At the time I could only assume that this was something that had a connection with Flo's feelings of disappointment. An article appearing in the *West Meath Examiner* some days after my investigation confirmed that my feelings were correct.

I had no doubt whatsoever that everything being done at the distillery would be successful because of the wonderful people there who were working hard in this earthly life and were being helped by a spirit family called the Lockes. They were pushing them still and wishing them well.

I would like to thank Bernadette and Brian Quinn for their kindness and hospitality during my visit to Locke's Distillery. I would also like to recommend that if you happen to be visiting Ireland and are around Kilbeggan, you take the opportunity to see for yourself what a whiskey distillery is all about. You never know – whiskey may not be the only spirit you will experience!

CHAPTER FIFTEEN

An Old Theatre

Over the past few years I have visited many theatres during my bi-annual tours around the country, appearing on stages through Ireland and the United Kingdom. I have also been involved in investigating a number of theatres, the most famous of which I think would be the Theatre Royal in Drury Lane, London, in the days when I was the resident medium with *Most Haunted*.

Contrary to popular belief, however, the Theatre Royal was not the first theatre I had investigated for a television programme. During my days with Granada Breeze, the then satellite arm of Granada Television, I had been involved with the programme *Predictions with*

Derek Acorah. The format of this programme would involve me demonstrating mediumship to a studio audience and then conducting a one-to-one reading with an individual who had telephoned in to request a 'sitting' with me. The third segment was comprised of a short pre-recorded film of me being taken out by the production staff to a location unknown to me for an investigation. I never knew what to expect when we did this. I would arrive at the studios in Manchester on the morning of the filming and would then be driven to wherever it was that the production team had decided would be suitable. One of those locations was the Lyceum Theatre in Crewe.

That day I had arrived in Manchester early in the morning. I had not been told to pack an overnight bag, so I knew that on this occasion the travel and filming would be completed that day. As I sat in the back of the car I wondered in which direction we would be heading. Would it be north, south, east or west?

After about an hour or more, I noticed that we were heading in the direction of Crewe. Eventually we reached the town. I wondered where on Earth we could be going. I couldn't see any old houses, castles or buildings that would make for a lively investigation into paranormal activity.

We eventually pulled into a car park. 'Come on, Derek,' the producer said to me, 'we'll take you to the place we've chosen for you today.'

We walked along a couple of streets and finally arrived at the door to the Lyceum Theatre.

As we entered the theatre I could sense immediately that apart from being quite old itself, this place held many more residual energies. I asked the manager whether she could show me around the building before I commenced my investigation.

Together we walked around the foyer, where I caught a whiff of lavender-scented perfume, and on through the auditorium to the stage. We exited the stage via the wings and slowly walked up and down the backstage corridors. I peered into each of the dressing rooms as we went along. The residual energies here were strong, with excitement and anticipation lying heavy in the air, apart from in one room. In this I detected a feeling of deep sadness and despondency.

As we slowly retraced our steps to the foyer, where coffee was waiting, I was satisfied that the trip had not been wasted, as I had managed to pick up on the residual energy within the theatre.

After that welcome cup of coffee, it was time to commence my investigation of the Lyceum Theatre. I concentrated on the atmosphere I had noticed when I had walked through the front door. Standing in the foyer, I closed my eyes and blocked out the hum of the passing traffic. I allowed my mind to clear and open to the energies contained within the building.

As we began our walk around, a picture formed in my mind's eye, but it was not of a theatre at all. I could see a church, with people walking into it. They were not attired in the fashions of today – the women wore long dresses and bonnets and the men were wearing 'Sunday best' trousers and coats. These people were not well dressed and were obviously members of the less fortunate section of society. I could also see a graveyard to the side of the church with gravestones set in rows.

I was sure that what I was seeing was something that no longer existed, and had the distinct impression that the Lyceum Theatre had been built on a burial site. I was more than pleased to note that there seemed to be no negativity in the building as a result of this.

Although I was told later that a very unhappy monk was alleged to haunt the area below the auditorium, I didn't pick up anything of his presence during my investigation. Perhaps his spirit visits the site from time to time, unhappy because the ground where his beloved church once stood has been put to a use that he would certainly not agree with, but when I was there he chose not to appear.

The crew and I continued our walk around the old theatre. As we made our way through the labyrinth of corridors typical of any old theatre, I detected a smell of smoke. Clairaudiently, I could hear a crackling blaze. Had the building been razed to the ground by fire at one time? The manager nodded. The theatre had indeed been the victim of a blaze in 1910 and the building had been completely destroyed.

We found ourselves back on the stage once more. I was not entirely surprised to pick up on the energies of circus people there. I knew that it had not been uncommon in the past for circuses to make appearances at such venues. The residual energies of the performing animals, the acrobats and jugglers were all there at Crewe, giving any medium a glimpse of past performances.

I can only describe theatres as sponges for psychic energies. It is because of the deep emotions displayed by the thespians as they portray their characters on the stage.

Snatches of deeply emotive speeches and the swish of ornate costumes now bombarded my senses. The scent of greasepaint hung heavy in the air. I stood centre-stage and drank in the atmosphere. I could feel anticipation and expectation, both drifting up from the audience area and on the stage itself. There was a fluttery sensation in my stomach as I picked up on the nervous excitement of the players.

As I stood there, my eye was drawn to a movement in a box high up at the side of the stage. A spirit man was standing there, dressed in the dark cloak and tall top hat of the evening dress of the late nineteenth century. He did not move or communicate with me, but merely stood and watched the stage. No doubt he was recalling the days when he either visited the theatre or appeared upon the stage himself.

'Do you see anything else?' Rachel urged.

I turned and looked at her. I could tell she was expecting more.

'No,' I replied, 'nothing more.'

Although the residual energy of the theatre was rich in memories, people from the world of spirit were on that day very sparse.

'What a pity. I thought you might find the ghost of a ballerina who hanged herself here,' Rachel said.

I looked around me. There was nothing there. Neither could I pick up the energies of deep sadness that would accompany such a terrible end.

'I doubt very much whether anybody committed suicide on this stage,' I told Rachel.

I went on to explain that I can never command or demand that spirit people return, just because we require them to do so. They are not performers and do not work to scripts. If they return to a location, they do so because they want to and for no other reason. In cases where there are grounded spirits, i.e. spirit people who have not moved away from this physical Earth, then the likelihood of a medium communicating with them is strong. In the case of spirit visitation, however, a medium – and anybody else – is purely at the mercy of spiritual whim. Spirits come and go as they please, but I knew that from time to time some of them still attended performances at the Lyceum Theatre, Crewe.

CHAPTER SIXTEEN

A Loving Family

Marina had been happily married for almost 39 years to George when illness struck and he suddenly passed over to the spirit world. Naturally Marina missed him, as they had enjoyed a loving and close relationship. It was with deep sadness in her heart that she followed George's coffin in to the church on the day of his funeral and said her last goodbyes to the man who had shared her life for so long.

George and Marina had a daughter named Trisha and, together with her small daughters Emma and Zoë, she comforted her mother in the difficult days following her father's funeral, but her home was in Ontario, Canada, many thousands of miles away. In spite of the distance, Marina and George had kept in close contact with their daughter and had visited her, her husband Neil and their two granddaughters at least once a year. The little girls had been extremely fond of their grandfather and they had all been a very close family indeed. Now Marina dreaded the day when Trisha would return to her own home, taking her daughters with her.

There was a further reason why Marina was not looking forward to Trisha's departure. She had begun to have strange experiences and was distressed at the thought of being left alone to cope with them. When retiring to bed at night, she had begun to see strange shapes and lights. The lights were brilliantly coloured and of dazzling clarity. She had also noticed, as she moved around her home, that she could smell acrid aroma tobacco and yet nobody in the house smoked cigarettes. She could even detect the smell of whisky in the air, but nobody ever took a drink of alcohol in the house. If she was sitting in a chair at night reading, with her daughter and the girls fast asleep up in their bedrooms, she would sometimes hear noises – small bangs and clicks, almost as though doors were being opened and closed, and the sound of footsteps on the stairs. It had reached a point where she was almost afraid to go to bed. When she did pluck up the courage, she found that she had difficulty falling asleep, as she was always listening for the next noise, or maybe for an unseen hand to open her bedroom door.

As the day of Trisha's departure drew nearer, Marina saw an article about me in the local newspaper. She decided to attempt to contact me by writing to the editor and asking him to pass her letter on to me. She wrote that she was sorry to bother me because she was sure that I was tremendously busy, but that she was overcome with nervousness at the thought of being left alone in her home. I could do nothing other than take pity on the poor lady.

A day or two later I arrived at Marina's home. She answered the door to me straight away and showed me into her sitting room, where Trisha was waiting to meet me. Marina had informed her of her experiences and her intention of writing to me and she was happy to agree to anything that would make her beloved mother feel calm and at peace in her own home once she had returned to her life in Canada.

The moment I walked into the room I could detect the spirit presence of a man. He was of medium height and quite tubby around the middle. His hair was grey and thinning, and he had a jovial smile on his face. I knew that this was the recently departed George. I was surprised at how strongly he was able to manifest in view of the short time since his passing to the spirit world. Usually it will take some months before a spirit person is able to gather sufficient energies to manifest in such a vigorous manner.

I was also able to detect that George wasn't the only visitor from the spirit world. In fact I would say that quite a number of family members had come along through the links of love in order to watch over Marina. They were all very much aware of how alone she would be feeling, as she had depended on George so much during his lifetime. She naturally doted on Trisha and her granddaughters, but George had been the mainstay of her life.

Marina invited me to take a seat. I could sense that she had a deep-seated belief system and knew almost as strongly as I did that we all live on after physical death. I had no hesitation therefore in telling her that her beloved George was with her. I also told her that George wasn't the only spirit person to have been in her home.

'Remember the grandfather who smoked those smelly cigarettes?' I asked her. 'And Granny Holmes who liked a drop of Scotch before she went to bed? She always used to tell you that it helped her sleep.'

Marina laughed. 'Yes, I remember,' she said, 'especially Granny. It wasn't just before she went to bed that she enjoyed her whisky!' I saw a light begin to dawn in her eyes. 'So that's why I've been smelling the tobacco and the whisky!' she exclaimed. 'Of course! Why didn't I realize?'

It often happens that when loved ones visit us from the world of spirit they will make us aware of their presence by permeating the atmosphere with an aroma of something that we would immediately link with them during their time with us here in the physical world. It is common for people to smell tobacco, a favourite scent, the smell of favoured flowers or cooking – anything, in fact, which would link a person in spirit to the family member they are visiting.

'And there was another George.' I looked at Marina expectantly. 'He came to collect your George at the time of his passing. I believe the second George would have had some type of heart problem, though he passed away quite unexpectedly after pneumonia set in.'

Marina's eyes lit up. 'That was my George's father,' she told me.

'And there's a lovely lady called Ivy. She's quite short and plump with white hair. She was there assisting George in his transition too. She drops in to say hello.'

Marina told me that Ivy had been George's sister. She had passed away as a result of stomach cancer some two years prior to George's own passing.

One by one, spirit people showed themselves in Marina's sitting room. George's mother, Marina's own mother and father and many others all came. The most special to Marina was a small spirit girl. She appeared to be no more than four or five years of age. I had to listen very carefully to make sure that I had not mistaken her name. 'She's telling me Maria,' I informed Marina. 'Almost like your name, but not quite … and she looks like you too.'

Tears appeared in Marina's eyes. 'That's my little girl,' she told me, 'my lovely, lovely little daughter. She was Trisha's older sister and we lost her when she was only five. She was knocked down by a car and although we prayed for her to pull through, she didn't. Trisha doesn't remember her at all, because she was only six months old at the time.'

I was more than happy to tell Marina that her little girl was safe and well and in the company of her family. She was grown now in the world of spirit and was a fine young lady.

It is rare that a person is blessed with so much spiritual presence around them. Marina's family were all coming to pay their respects to her and to tell her that she wasn't alone. Hadn't she noticed their efforts to let her know that they were around her, guarding and keeping her safe?

Marina was rather shame-faced at not having recognized their attempts at communication. 'I was frightened and not thinking properly,' she told me. 'What with losing George and the thought of Trisha going with the girls, I just didn't think at all. I thought it was something evil going on.'

I stood up to leave. I had done nothing more than calm the fears of a lady who, through fear of living on her own for the first time in many years, had been interpreting every noise and creak as something negative and untoward.

As she shook my hand at the doorway she thanked me profusely. 'I won't be afraid now Derek. I know that everybody's around me and that I needn't fear anything. Trisha has told me that when she gets back to Canada, she's going to arrange for me to spend six months of each year living with her and her family. I'll come back to England for part of the year to spend time with my spirit family, but for the rest of the year I'll be with my lovely daughter and granddaughters.'

I laughed and told her that it didn't matter where she went or how far she travelled, her spirit family would always be with her.

CHAPTER SEVENTEEN

Victoria Baths

In my time as an investigative medium I have been to some very strange places, but none stranger than a location I was taken to by the production team for Granada Breeze's *Predictions with Derek Acorah*.

When we pulled up outside the building I first thought the lead car had taken a wrong turning and that we were merely pulling in to turn around and retrace our route. However, I was wrong. Engines were switched off and the crew began unloading their equipment. I was curious as to what type of building this was – what secrets it would hold. I looked up and saw something etched into the stonework: a swimming baths! What on Earth was I doing here?

We approached the door, which was opened for us by a lady who was obviously in attendance. As we walked in, I was struck by the marvellously intricate dark green tiling that covered the walls to shoulder height. There was a ticket booth to the left with a turnstile-type entrance. Although I had never visited these premises before, everything about the entrance hall seemed familiar to me. Then I realized that I had been to an old swimming baths before. It was in Liverpool, in an area named Newsham Park.

The swimming baths in Liverpool had been bought by a company who supplied and sold Koi carp. Koi are a passion for me. I love to watch them. I'm fascinated by their grace and colour. Watching them as they swim around in a garden pond on a still, warm summer's evening is just about the most peaceful scenario I can think of. I have spent many hours meditating whilst sitting next to my garden pond. The movement of the fish, the colours and the sound of the trickling water and the stillness of the countryside are hugely calming and inspirational.

On one occasion I had seen an advertisement in a local newspaper for some Koi. A company in Newsham Park had imported fresh stock and I had gone along to see whether they had anything that would appeal to me. I had been amazed at how the company had utilized the old swimming baths. Instead of being full of bathers, the huge baths were full of Koi carp and other breeds of fish, and the showers and cubicles were now home to rabbits, guinea pigs and mice. Exotic birds on stands or in large cages filled the entrance hall. It was an amazing place. However, I digress.

I could see that the swimming baths in Manchester were old and I guessed they dated back 100 years or so. I was fascinated to see that there were signs for 'Males' and 'Females'. Obviously, in those days mixed bathing had been frowned upon. In fact, not only had the genders been segregated, but the classes had also been kept apart in the case of the men, as there were notices stating 'Males 1st Class' and 'Males 2nd Class'.

We walked through to the 'Males 2nd Class' swimming bath, now lying empty and bare. I had the definite impression that at one time there would have been bathing cubicles around the edge of the huge room. I remembered that when the baths were created, they weren't just there for the fun of swimming and cavorting around in the water but had the very necessary function of providing washing facilities for families who did not have bathrooms in their homes. In central Manchester very few people would have owned such a luxury. They would, of necessity (and indeed if they had the money and inclination to do so) have trooped along as a family to avail themselves of hot water, soap and a clean towel, all for the price of a copper or two.

I looked up and saw a galleried section that contained more cubicles. At one time each cubicle would have been equipped with a partial door, but now some of the doors had disappeared completely. Some remained, but most were held on by a single creaking and rusty hinge.

I opened myself up to the atmosphere of the place. Immediately I was taken back to a time when the baths would have been full of hustle and bustle, of men swimming in their archaic bathing suits and teaching their sons how to swim. It was a pleasant and friendly atmosphere. Clairvoyantly, I could see men coming and going in the cubicles set around the side of the pool. Billowing steam belched from the hot water supplied to facilitate their bathing. Clairaudiently, I could hear the murmur of conversation between men who obviously knew one another from their weekly bathing. The shouts of boys of all ages echoed around. The more adept of the lads jumped and splashed into the pool. Occasionally a shout of irritation could be heard as an enthusiastic youngster cut across the path of a dedicated adult swimmer. In fact, apart from the wash baths, the scene was very similar to a swimming baths of today – apart from the fact that there were no girls or women there at all.

The scene I had opened up to was all residual energy held within the fabric of the old building. So far I had detected no spirit presence at all, merely the sights and sounds of an afternoon at the swimming baths. I did, however, receive the impression that an accident had taken place in the area. I couldn't pick up anything that would suggest a passing to the world of spirit, but there was definitely the residual energy of great trauma involving a young boy.

We moved on to the 'Males 1st Class' section. Here it was a different picture altogether. Far grander than the previous swimming pool, this room was tiled from floor to ceiling and had strikingly ornate stained-glass windows. I felt that at one time the woodwork would have been highly polished but unfortunately now it all was looking rather dreary. Still, at one time, it was obvi- ous that opulence had been the byword.

This pool also had a galleried section, but here, instead of more cubicles intended to accommodate private washing, there were rows of seats. It seemed that at some time this pool had been used for demonstrations of diving and swimming.

It was with some consternation that I heard something one would not normally link with swimming baths, and that was the sound of music. I can only describe it as 'Big Band' music. I could see couples dancing, whirling around to the music. My curiosity got the better of me and so I turned to the guide who was accompanying us and told her what I was hearing.

'Oh yes, Derek,' she replied, 'that doesn't surprise me at all. They used to cover this pool up with boards and hold dances here.' She laughed. 'There's many a romance been started in the old Victoria Baths!'

I walked down into the now empty bathing pool. As I walked around I had the oddest feeling that some type of fantasy had been acted out here. I was bemused and could not quite understand what I was being given. 'Help me, Sam,' I asked.

I could hear Sam laughing in the background. 'It was a story, Derek,' he told me. 'A film was made here. Don't confuse truth with fiction,' he warned.

The old baths were indeed full of surprises – from Friday night ablutions to swimming for pleasure to film-making! There was a mass of residual energy, but only the briefest of spirit presence, and that was a man. I would say that he would have been in his early to middle forties. He was wearing a uniform and appeared to be very officious. I could see him striding around the area of the swimming baths in a pompous manner. He was obviously a person who had been employed to ensure that nobody misbehaved or went too far in their water larks.

On we went to another area. This time I could pick up only the residual energy of women. 'This must have been the ladies' bathing area,' I announced.

I could sense the light-heartedness and happiness of mothers with their children enjoying the gentle warmth of the water. From the stalls at the side I glimpsed the poorer women attending their children at their weekly bath. I could see large copper jugs with wisps of steam rising from them as the attendants ferried hot water to and fro. It was a gentle scene, but one that was now long gone.

Try as I might, I could summon up no more spirit energy. Once again I was aware that no matter how much a medium may want to, they cannot command a spirit presence. The people who had enjoyed the old baths at Salford were happy to continue their lives in the world of spirit. The only person who chose to be in visitation that day was the old attendant, returning to continue his duties from beyond the veil.

Chapter Eighteen

The Man Who Couldn't Say No

Like most couples, Gwen and I enjoy a spot of shopping. One day we decided that rather than visit our home town of Southport, we would travel a little further afield and drive over to the Trafford Centre in Manchester. We got into the car and arrived at our destination around mid-morning.

We had been at the shopping centre for something short of a couple of hours when we decided that it was time for lunch. After finding a table in the food area, we settled down with a sandwich and a cup of coffee. We were both enjoying ourselves. It was a rare treat to spend time in each other's company without having people along with us.

After we had finished our lunch we resumed walking leisurely around, popping into a shop when we spied something interesting in the window. It was whilst we were strolling along that we heard the sound of running feet. We turned and saw a woman rushing towards us. She almost knocked me off my feet as she grabbed hold of my arm.

'Derek Acorah!' she almost screamed. 'It is you, isn't it?'

I agreed that I was indeed Derek Acorah.

'Oh, I'm sorry! Did I nearly knock you over? I was that surprised, I just had to speak to you.'

I smiled to myself. I will never understand why sometimes people are surprised that I take part in the usual daily pastimes common to all. I think some people are of the opinion that I live in a cupboard under the stairs and only come out when it is dark. They cannot comprehend that I do the normal everyday things in a normal everyday manner.

'I think I must have been meant to bump into you today, Derek,' the woman continued. 'Have you got five minutes to spare?'

I said that I did.

'Should we sit down over here?' she asked, gesturing towards a bench situated on the concourse.

We walked over to the bench and sat down. The woman introduced herself as Sheila and she had a harrowing tale to tell.

Sheila told me that she was married for 26 years to a man whom she described as 'little better than a monster'. 'You won't believe what that man did to me over the years,' she told me. 'He beat me black and blue and made my life hell. Of course the problem was the drink – he couldn't say no to it. It didn't matter what it was or whose it was, he'd drink it.'

I wondered out loud why she hadn't gone along to the police to report her husband's behaviour.

'He used to threaten that he'd kill me if I or the kids told anybody what was going on,' she said.

I didn't quite understand why Sheila was telling me all this, but continued to listen.

Eventually Sheila's husband had fallen ill. 'He didn't last long,' she said. 'One minute he was here and the next he was gone. It's a terrible thing to admit, but all I could feel was relief. I didn't love him – or at least I hadn't loved him for many a long year. I just got down on my knees and thanked God for taking him away. Was that a terrible thing to do, d'you think, Derek?'

I had to say that perhaps it was not such a terrible thing to wish to be free from a person who was making life so intolerable.

'The thing is, Derek,' Sheila confided, 'Dougie – that was his name, Dougie – didn't want to be cremated. He always wanted to be buried next to his mam, but because he'd been a bastard to me virtually all the time I'd known him, I decided, "Sod you, mate! You're going up in smoke!" And so that's what I did – I had him cremated.'

It was apparently after she had come back after Dougie's cremation ceremony that things had started happening in the house.

'It's as though something's come from hell to haunt me,' she said. 'In fact, I'd swear that it's Dougie come back!'

She told me that she could not sleep without leaving the lights on at night and would not entertain sleeping in the bed that she had once shared with her husband. Instead she remained downstairs, using the sofa as her bed.

'I know it's an awful lot to ask of you and your wife, but would you be able to come to my house to see if you can tell me whether Dougie's there or not?' she pleaded.

I looked at Gwen, who nodded in a resigned sort of a way.

'OK,' I told Sheila. 'It's not something I would normally do, but we'll come to your house for a few minutes. It will have to be now, though. Tomorrow I'm off again down south to do some filming.'

Sheila was ecstatic. 'Thank you so much, both of you,' she said.

We left the shopping centre and followed Sheila to her vehicle. After telling her to wait where she was for us, we returned to our own car and then met up with her once more. We drove out of the shopping centre and, following Sheila's car, drove for some 20 minutes before turning into a quiet cul-de-sac. We pulled up outside Sheila's house.

Sheila led us inside. Immediately I entered the home I could feel an oppressive atmosphere. We almost jumped out of our skins when we heard the door of an upstairs room slam violently shut.

Sheila took us through to her lounge. As I entered the room, I tripped and almost fell. It was almost as though an unseen person had stuck their foot out and tripped me personally. The negative energy in the room was immediately apparent to me.

'I know you're around, Dougie,' I announced. As I did so, a framed photograph of Sheila that was standing on the television tipped forward and fell to the floor. A low disembodied chuckle could be heard by all three of us.

Sheila invited Gwen and me to sit down. I mentally asked Sam to come close to me to protect not only me but also Gwen and Sheila. I was beginning to regret bringing my wife into such an atmosphere. She is well used to watching me work, having accompanied me on hundreds of investigations, but it's very rarely that I involve her in the type of rescue work that I now knew confronted me.

A man's voice grated in my ear. 'The bitch! She tried to poison me!'

I looked at Sheila in surprise. I asked her why Dougie would accuse her of such a thing.

She responded in a shocked tone, 'But he died of natural causes! Admittedly, it was due to his heavy drinking, but it was his own fault.'

Dougie's nasty tones answered her. 'I heard her,' he said, 'plotting and planning with the doctor – all their talk about poisoning when they were standing next to my hospital bed!'

I repeated what Dougie had to say to Sheila. 'But the doctor was talking about *alcohol* poisoning,' she told me in surprise. 'Dougie had poisoned *himself* by drinking too much alcohol. That's why he died!'

'And that business about burning me too!' Dougie growled. 'I'll never forgive her for that! She knew I wanted to be buried next to my mother. I'm going nowhere! I'll stay and make her life a misery till it's her time and then I'll show her what's what.'

It was evident that Dougie was totally confused. And he had not allowed himself to progress properly to the spirit world so that his loved ones on the higher side of life could explain to him the error of his earthly ways. He had shunned his guides and helpers and was determined to remain close to the Earth's atmosphere. Admittedly, this wasn't helped by the fact that Sheila had cremated his earthly remains rather than have him buried with his mother. This, I am afraid, was a human failing on Sheila's part, but she hardly deserved to have Dougie continue to treat her badly after his passing over.

I asked Sheila and Gwen to join me in prayer and to ask their guides and helpers to draw close. We needed spiritual strength in the room in order to dissipate the negativity that Dougie's presence was creating. I prayed to Dougie's own guides and helpers to come once more and surround him with their love and compassion. I communicated with Dougie himself on a mental level, pleading with him to allow himself to be led away to the heavenly state where he could begin his progression through the spiritual realms.

Dougie was afraid. 'I'm not being taken to hell, am I?' he asked me.

I told him that he wouldn't be going to the lower realms, but would be taken to a place where he could begin to recover from the ravages of his addiction and learn that the manner in which he had conducted his physical lifetime was not correct. He would be taken to a place of learning and helped by his own guides and helpers to recover and to forgive Sheila for not respecting his wishes. He would learn that we all suffer as a consequence of our actions. 'What goes around comes around!'

Then I saw a bright light build in the room. It was as though the area was filled with the love and peace of angelic beings.

'Go forward, my friend,' I uttered over and over again.

The atmosphere in the room became lighter and lighter. With relief, I knew that Dougie had been collected by his loved ones in spirit and taken to a place where he could commence his true progress.

Sheila picked up the photograph that had fallen from the top of the television. 'It seems so much calmer in here now,' she said. 'That horrible atmosphere has gone. I almost feel sorry for Dougie, you know. He was never happy; he was always in such black moods because of the drinking. I suppose it was a depression of sorts. He never enjoyed life.'

It was a very sad situation. I felt so much for Sheila who had suffered at the hands of a man who was not truly bad but who had allowed himself to be controlled by alcohol. That awful addiction had ruined not only his own life but his wife's as well.

Sheila thanked me profusely as Gwen and I made our way out of her home. 'I'll let you know whether he comes back, Derek,' she told me as she waved us off.

True to her word, a week or two later, Sheila telephoned me. She told me that nothing untoward had happened in her home since the day of my visit. In fact she had found that the atmosphere had become peaceful.

Not only that, her fortunes had turned for the better. Whereas once she had considered that she had no luck at all, now everything had changed. She had won some money, and a job on her home that she had been badgering the council about for a long, long while had been started at last. She had also met up with a friend she hadn't seen for years and, their circumstances being similar in that they were both widowed, they were now enjoying nights out together and were planning a holiday.

'I feel so much better,' she told me. 'It's almost as though Dougie is wishing me well.'

I agreed that it could well be that Dougie was influencing her life from the heavenly side of life in a positive way.

'I've made a decision, too,' Sheila continued. 'I've been feeling guilty about not having Dougie buried with his mother, as he wished, and there's nothing I can do about the cremation, but I've decided to take his ashes to the cemetery and arrange for them to be buried in his mother's grave.'

I was positive that Dougie would approve of Sheila's decision, even though he would now realize that our physical remains mean absolutely nothing. However, it was a gesture that he would appreciate and I am sure that the end of Sheila's negative feelings towards him would speed his progress towards a truly heavenly state.

CHAPTER NINETEEN

Land of the Pharaohs

As I flew into Cairo airport, darkness had already fallen. As I looked out of the plane window I could see the strobe lights playing over the face of the Great Pyramid, illuminating it with an eerie bluey-green glow. Behind it I could make out the shapes of two more pyramids in the reflected lighting.

Although I had visited the Giza pyramids, said to represent the sun-god Ra, once before, it had only been a very short trip. Now I was looking forward to realizing the dream I had held since that day – to return to Egypt and conduct an investigation of one of the greatest civilizations the world has ever known.

Sam had always promised me that I would fulfil this dream, but at times I had wondered how this would come about. He had always responded to my musings by whispering quietly, 'Wait! Be patient. It will happen.'

Once more he had been proved correct. I had been approached by Paul Flexton of Ruggie Media, the company who had produced *Derek Acorah's Ghost Towns*, who had asked whether I would be interested in travelling to Lower Egypt for a month to film a series of eight programmes. This would involve investigating, from a medium's viewpoint, the mysteries and myths surrounding the land of the pharaohs. Needless to say, I readily agreed. The presenter of the programme was to be Tessa Dunlop.

It was planned that we would spend the first three days in Cairo itself and then travel down to Luxor, home to the Valley of the Kings and the Valley of the Queens. We would then continue travelling south, following the route of the river Nile to Al-Minya before returning north once more to Giza and then going back to Cairo before returning home a month later. Ramy Romany, our fixer, had organized our hotels and the routes we would follow for the duration of our stay in the country.

If anybody has not visited Egypt but is even the tiniest bit interested in knowing more about the ancient civilization of the pharaohs, I would definitely recommend at least one trip to the country. Egypt is fascinating. In some places it is up to the minute, modern and fast moving, and in others, away from the cities and the tourist spots, it is just as it must have been thousands of years ago.

Our investigations began at the Cairo Museum of Antiquities. I had visited it on an earlier trip to the city, but I was unprepared for the surprises in store. Tessa, the crew and I were privileged to be allowed into areas not normally open to the public. Anybody who watches LivingTV's *Paranormal Egypt* will, I am sure, be fascinated by our findings.

Our next port of call was Luxor where, passing the giant sentinels of the two Colossi of Memnon, we visited the Valley of the Kings and the Valley of the Queens in the Theban hills, including KV no. 62, the burial place of Tutankhamun, the famous boy king. His golden death mask needs no introduction. That mask is now in the museum at Cairo, although the pharaoh's mummy, together with its outer golden casing, still resides in its sarcophagus in the original burial chamber.

I was amazed to see that although he was possibly one of the most famous of all the Egyptian kings, Tutankhamun's burial shaft that was not nearly as deep or as ornately decorated as those of previous kings' tombs. It was explained to me that as soon as a pharaoh ascended the throne, work began on his tomb. If he remained in office for a long time, then the ornate paintings and hieroglyphics were likely to be completed. Should he pass away at an early age, as Tutankhamun did, he would be buried straightaway, regardless of whether the work on the tomb had been completed or not.

Before each tomb was sealed, the body of the pharaoh would be bedecked with gold and jewels and surrounded by numerous treasures and items that he would need for their journey to the afterlife. The majority of tombs were robbed in antiquity and the only one that has so far been discovered intact is that of Tutankhamun. It remained untouched until Howard Carter made his miraculous discovery in 1922.

The only queen to be buried in the Valley of the Kings was Hatshepsut and we travelled to her temple in order to investigate the story behind the great queen.

Apparently it was impossible for a woman to be named a pharaoh and so when claiming the throne Hatshepsut declared herself a man.

It was close to Hatshepsut's temple that I came face to face with the local donkeys. It had been decided that the whole crew would ride them up a trail to achieve some spectacular scenery footage. I am not known for my horse-riding, let alone my expertise on a donkey, and my first attempt saw me slipping right over the donkey and onto the floor on the other side. On my second attempt, however, I managed to stay in the saddle for the duration of the outward journey. I was feeling quite pleased with myself, but when I climbed onto the donkey's back for the return journey, it decided enough was enough. No amount of pulling or pushing would make the poor beast move.

Ray was beside himself with laughter. 'I *told* you you'd put on weight, Ackers!' he chortled. 'I could tell by the way the donkey's eyes went like Betty Boop's the minute you climbed on its back!'

I resigned myself to walking back down the hill on my own two feet, whilst making a mental note that I would definitely lose some weight when I arrived home back in England.

The episode had reminded me very much of a visit to Dubai some years earlier, when a camel had refused to rise to its feet once I had climbed onto its back. I am happy to report, though, that the camels in Egypt are far more amenable and I was able to enjoy the splendour of the Giza pyramids from the vantage-point of a fully standing camel.

There were so many memorable moments. At the tombs of the nobles and the workers' village at Deir al-Medinah, it was exceedingly hot and the only respite was to enter the tombs. Deir al-Medinah was where the masons, painters and decorators who created the tombs lived. They were sworn to secrecy about the location of the tombs they were working on, as it was feared that if word was passed around, the tombs would be robbed as soon as a pharaoh was buried.

We then turned our attention to the temples of Karnak and Madinat Habu. Karnak is situated on the eastern side of the river Nile, whilst Madinat Habu, the mortuary temple of Rameses III, is on the west side. The temple at Karnak, otherwise known as 'The Most Select of Places', was perhaps the most important religious site in Egyptian history. The temple area contains a sacred lake guarded by the top of one of the two obelisks placed there by Queen Hatshepsut.

A mile or so down the road, running alongside the Nile, is the Luxor temple. Although no investigation was carried out at this location, Ray and I took time out to take a walk around this fascinating site during a break in filming. In the evening, light shows are held here, but unfortunately, because of our work schedule, we were unable to experience this marvel.

The temple at Luxor was once also guarded by two enormous obelisks. Only one remains. The other now stands in the centre of Paris, having been taken from Luxor by the engineer Lebas in 1833 and relocated at Place de la Concorde in 1836. As we approached the temple by walking down the long avenue flanked by sphinxes with human heads, I was experiencing a feeling of expectation.

Ray and I wandered in and out the columns topped with capitals in the form of open papyrus flowers, admiring the view of the temple with the minaret of the mosque of Abu-el-Haggag in the background. It was exceedingly hot and after about 30 minutes we stopped in a shaded area for a rest and to avail ourselves of the bottled water we had brought with us.

Whilst I was resting, I noticed that I still had the sense of anticipation. I knew that there was a very strong spiritual presence around in the atmosphere and almost felt as though we were being followed by an unseen being.

Ray turned to me. 'Can you smell that perfume, Derek?'

Sure enough, the air was scented. It was a beautiful smell and unlike anything I had experienced before. I was sure that we were surrounded by spiritual energy. I expanded my consciousness but could pick up nothing other than a feeling of great spiritual energy.

Refreshed, Ray and I began to wander round again. We entered a room that had remained intact. Hieroglyphics were painted on the walls and the deep blue of the ceiling was dotted with a pattern of stars designed to resemble the sky at night.

As I stood in the centre of the room looking up at it, I felt that something had been placed over my head and shoulders. In spite of the heat outside, I began to feel cooler and then almost cold.

Ray, who had been examining the hieroglyphics, turned round. 'Hey, Derek, you look as though you're shivering!' he exclaimed.

As Ray spoke I felt what seemed to be almost like a bolt shoot into my back. I straightened up suddenly, arching my spine against the force of the spirit being who was trying to close in on my aura. I gasped as I sent out thoughts to Sam, asking him to protect me and put an end to this onslaught.

Gradually the pressure that I was experiencing eased somewhat. Whoever it was that had been trying to overshadow me had obviously been persuaded otherwise by Sam.

'Are you alright?' Ray asked me. I told him that I was fine and that he shouldn't worry. With that, he wandered out of the room and went to look at an adjoining area some yards away.

I was still very much aware that the room was full of spiritual energies. I remained there, fascinated by what I was experiencing. Although I didn't want to be overshadowed by a spirit being, I knew that there was something yet for me to experience.

Then I heard a noise coming from the corner of the room. I looked over and saw, to my surprise, the spirit form of my grandmother. She didn't speak to me, merely smiled, put her hands together as though in prayer and then faded from my sight. I didn't understand why she would be showing herself to me in the middle of a temple in Egypt.

A few moments later, as I was about to walk out of the room and continue my wanderings, I heard another noise. I turned and looked back into the room. Near the back wall, the spirit form of a man was building up rapidly. He was obviously of ancient times, as he was adorned with the robes I had seen in the many pictures of ancient Egypt. From his stance and bearing I could tell that he had been a very powerful man during his time on Earth and I knew without question that he was still exceedingly powerful in a spiritual sense.

An overwhelmingly good feeling filled the room. The spirit man stared at me serenely, then raised his arm and pointed at me. He then lifted his hand to his face and put his finger on a point in the middle of his forehead, as though in recognition of the third eye.

I heard Sam's voice. 'He is letting you know that he was the same as you when he walked this Earth 4,000 years ago. He was a man of greatness. He knows about our time in Ethiopia and he is telling you that some 4,000 years ago you knew him in Egypt and you will meet again in a physical lifetime. He sends you his blessings and protection.'

I felt humbled. I understood now why my grandmother had shown herself. She was proud that such a highly evolved spirit being was about to visit me. I also now understood why I had always felt drawn to Egypt and its culture.

The atmosphere in the room changed once more, becoming stuffy and warm. The highly spiritual presence had departed.

I suddenly remembered that I had not been given his name. As I walked out of the room I mentally asked Sam what it was.

His reply was, 'In the future you will know. Now is not the correct time.'

I was surprised, but I had to accept what Sam had told me.

Ray was sitting on a large stone enjoying a cigarette. He handed me the packet. 'Alright, Ackers?' he asked.

'Yes,' I replied. 'I'm fine.'

'It's about time we jumped into a cab and got back to the location,' Ray continued. 'We've got more work to do.'

* * *

The next leg of our journey saw us flying back up north to Giza, the home of the famous pyramids. The staff at our hotel there, the Sofitel Le Sphinx, were extremely friendly and made us more than welcome. Whilst in Giza, we investigated the Sphinx, said to be in the likeness of the great pharaoh Khufu, and his pyramid, which lies directly behind the Sphinx. It was an exceedingly eerie feeling to know that whilst climbing first down then up the confined tunnel leading to the burial chamber of Khufu there were millions of tons of limestone above me.

From Giza we followed the banks of the Nile to Al-Minya, where there was an enormous Muslim cemetery known as the Corner of the Dead. The rows upon rows of mud-brick graves were amazing to see.

To reach Al-Amarnah, the location of our next investigation, where it is said that Akhenaten and his wife Nefertiti once stayed, we had to pass through the quaint town of Mallawi before crossing the Nile by means of a local ferry and travelling onward across the desert. This was almost like travelling back in a time machine. I doubt whether customs there have changed much in the past 2,000 years. The donkey was still the main mode of transport and people were still farming just as they had for millennia.

Crossing the Nile on the ferry was an experience in itself. The ferries were only very small affairs – flat boards with a small shelter on one side. Each one would accommodate, at a squeeze, four or five vehicles. It became a matter of much hilarity for us that no one would remain in the vehicles for the duration of the crossing, just in case they rolled forward and into the river below.

After completing our work in Al-Minya, we were more than overjoyed to wave a fond farewell to the mosquitoes that had shared our rather basic hotel bungalows on the banks of the Nile. We travelled back to Giza, looking forward to a proper bed, air conditioning that worked and a real shower.

It was when we arrived back in Giza that I had a day or two off from filming. I was exhausted by now and was looking forward to spending some time relaxing in the shade. It was June and the intense heat was not conducive to working the protracted hours that we had been doing. We had been doing early-morning shoots and sometimes working through to the afternoon, then having a few hours' break before resuming filming once darkness fell. On other occasions we would be up and about quite early in the morning and work through the heat of the day and well into the evening, sometimes arriving back at our hotel at midnight. We had been working almost non-stop for more than two weeks and my spiritual energies were drained.

'You look tired, sir,' the concierge of the hotel said to me one day.

I agreed that I was feeling very tired and said that although it would have been tempting to lie around the pool on a sun-lounger, it was far too hot to do so.

The concierge knew that the crew and I were involved in paranormal investigations and that I was a spirit medium. 'What you need is a boost to your energies,' he said. 'I know someone who can take you to the very person to help you.'

With that, he called a hotel driver over. 'This is Hassan,' he told me. 'He will take you to someone who can help you.'

I was intrigued. I went over to where Ray and Gwen were sitting and asked them whether they would like to accompany me. They both agreed. We met Hassan once more in the hotel reception and followed him outside to his car.

After driving for some 10 or 15 minutes, Hassan pulled up outside a rather unremarkable-looking building. He took us inside.

We waited for a few moments in a small foyer area before a door opened and a tall man stepped into the room. Immediately I saw him I recognized that he was a highly evolved spirit. His whole being seemed to light up the room, such was the force of his energy. Just being in his company made me feel more alive and invigorated.

'This is Mr Ibrahim,' Hassan said. No first name was offered.

Mr Ibrahim walked towards me and embraced me. In broken English he uttered the words, 'Welcome, brother! You are a like soul. Follow me.'

I looked back to Ray and Gwen. 'Do you mind if I go with him?' I asked them.

They said that I should go and do what I had to do and they would wait in the reception area for me.

Mr Ibrahim led me through a curtained doorway into a room full of beautiful murals and tapestry hangings. I was amazed. To one side of the room stood what I recognized as a physiotherapist's table. Behind this, the wall was covered with shelves full of bottles containing liquids of many different hues.

'First sit, my friend,' Mr Ibrahim said, gesturing me towards a chair. 'You have been working so very hard for the spirit and they know and appreciate this, but you have been spiritually beaten up. I can see this by your aura. You also need certain of your chakras cleansing, my friend. May I do this for you? You will work so much better later.'

I felt completely at ease in Mr Ibrahim's company. I knew that I was with someone who was like-minded. He understood the workings of spirit and recognized that I was mentally, physically and spiritually drained. To continue with my quest, I needed help. I agreed to let him conduct a chakra cleansing on me.

Chakras can also be described as 'energy centres'. Six of these centres are located along the spinal column and one is at the top of the head. From the top down, they are known as the crown, third eye, throat, heart, solar plexus, spleen and sacral chakras. It is the job of the chakras to draw in energy from the sun and the Earth, and if they are blocked, these streams of vitality and natural energy will not be absorbed. This is where chakra cleansing or clearing comes in. This procedure clears the way for a person to absorb these natural energies and gives a feeling of thorough relaxation and well-being to the individual concerned.

After taking off my shirt and my shoes, I lay down on the table. I closed my eyes and allowed Mr Ibrahim to do his work.

First I heard him utter what I assumed to be a prayer. This was said in Arabic, but from the tone of his voice I knew that Mr Ibrahim was communing with a higher spirit. After a moment or two I heard the rattle of glass on glass as he took a drop of oil from one bottle, a couple of drops from another bottle and so on until he seemed satisfied with the result. He mixed them together in a dish, then, using a small amount of the oils, he then anointed the seven chakra points of my body – the crown of my head, my forehead, my throat, my heart, my solar plexus, my abdomen and the base of my spine. Following that, he passed his hands backwards and forwards over these points. He was not touching me; his hands were an inch or two above my flesh.

On and on he worked, all the while communicating with his guides and helpers. I felt a great regenerative heat penetrating the key points of my body. I was deeply relaxed and almost drifted off to another plane.

After about ten minutes he stopped. I had never felt so euphoric and energized, whilst at the same time at peace.

'Rest there for a while, Derek,' he told me.

As I lay there I felt my consciousness opening. I moved to a place of great enlightenment. My eyes were closed, but the light was so bright that it was almost unbearable.

Clairaudiently, I heard a voice. I didn't recognize it at all, but it had a great calming quality.

'You do your work well,' it said. 'We approve of what you are doing and it was our influence that led you to Omar the spiritual master. We wish you well in your endeavours whilst you are here in Egypt. You are safe and well protected. Go about your work – we are with you. You will meet the spirits of some great people but they will not harm you. They cannot harm you. Go in peace, dear friend.'

Then silence fell again and I suppose I must have dozed off for a few minutes.

I was woken by the swish of the curtain covering the doorway being drawn back. I opened my eyes. Mr Ibrahim, or Omar as I now knew him, was standing beside the bed, a smile on his serene face. 'How are you feeling, Derek?' he asked.

I told him that I felt wonderful, and I did. I felt rejuvenated and invigorated. My tiredness had disappeared completely and I felt ready to face the world. I climbed off the bed, put on my shirt and shoes and followed Mr Ibrahim through to the reception area where Gwen and Ray were waiting for me.

I took my wallet out of my pocket to pay for the healing that I had received.

'No, no! I don't require payment – it was my duty to help you,' said Mr Ibrahim. 'All I ask is that you continue with your work for the world of spirit. Sometimes it is difficult and sometimes you may wish to give up, but the time is not right for that. You have much more work to do for the world of spirit, Derek.'

He finished by telling me that although I felt marvellous now, I would really feel the benefits of the cleansing after a good night's sleep.

I thanked him profusely. He had made a new man of me. Ray and Gwen couldn't believe that the tired and jaded person who had accompanied them into the building had been left behind in that small room, to be replaced by someone with real verve for life.

'You look chirpy,' Gwen remarked. 'What happened in there?'

'I'll tell you later,' I replied.

Hassan, who had waited for us, drove us back to the hotel.

Over a cup of coffee I regaled Gwen and Ray with what had happened during our visit to Mr Ibrahim. 'Well, whatever he did, it certainly worked!' they both remarked, laughing.

After our coffee we went to our rooms to shower and change for dinner. It was a rare luxury not having to get into working clothes, climb aboard the bus and go off to work at this time of the evening.

Gwen and I left our room to meet up with Ray in the hotel lounge. As we walked along the corridor I realized that I had left my wallet in the bedroom. Gwen said that she would go on to meet Ray whilst I went back for it.

As I pushed the door of our room open and walked in, I thought I heard a noise. I knew that it wouldn't be the hotel staff, as they had completed the cleaning long before. I closed the door behind me and looked round.

A spirit man was standing in the middle of the room. I could see him very clearly. From his robes I knew that he was a holy man. He slowly walked towards me. I stood rooted to the spot. I could sense that I was in no danger.

As the priestly figure reached me, he raised his arms and gently placed his hands upon my shoulders. I could feel the chill of his touch through my shirt. He then raised one of his hands and placed it on the top of my head. I felt a deep emotional peace. He then slowly dropped his hands and backed away from me.

He was uttering words in a language I did not understand, so I called out mentally to Sam. In a moment, though I couldn't see him, I was aware that he was with me.

'Who is this person and what is he saying?' I asked.

Sam told me that the man was a highly evolved person and had great spiritual strength. In his physical life 5,000 years ago he had been a high priest in Egypt. He had come to give me a blessing and I should be very honoured by it.

The spirit figure faded and I was alone once more. The bedroom felt very peaceful and pleasant now and I almost wanted to lie down on the bed and go to sleep. I realized, though, that Gwen and Ray were waiting for me. Reluctantly I picked up my wallet and walked to the reception to meet them.

This had been a wonderful day. Not only had I met a spiritual master of this physical world but I had also received the blessing of an ancient Egyptian high priest. I felt truly blessed.

The following morning, true to Mr Ibrahim's word, I woke early and felt more than ready to face the day. Never had I felt so alive and invigorated. I can truly say that a miracle was worked that day in Egypt.

It was time to go back to work once more, but with the help of Mr Ibrahim's ministrations, I was now fit and raring to go. The next location was Saqqara and the Step Pyramid, otherwise known as the Pyramid of Djoser, the oldest pyramid in Egypt. It is said that it is designed in such a way that the steps facilitate the pharaoh's journey into the afterlife. It was designed by Imhotep, the founder of Egyptian medicine. He was an exceptional man who was a noted astronomer as well as an architect, magician and great philosopher. In fact he has been likened to Thoth, the Egyptian god of learning.

It is believed that the tomb of Imhotep contains the oldest mummy in Egypt, but I don't believe the mummy in the sarcophagus is actually that of Imhotep.

It is my belief that his body is yet to be discovered, and during filming of the programme, I endeavoured to seek out the physical remains of this great man. This project is still ongoing.

From Saqqara we travelled to Memphis. After parking the vehicles at a couple of isolated buildings, we trudged through the hot Sahara sands to the Animal Galleries. Dr Zahi Hawass of Egyptian Council of Antiquities had given special permission for these to be opened so that an investigation could take place there. Entering the underground tomb, I was absolutely amazed to see thousands upon thousands of mummified remains of birds and small animals. Each body was encased in a small pottery sarcophagus. It was an amazing experience, during which I picked up the essence of a guardian of the tomb.

Our final location for filming was the workers' village close to the Great Pyramid. I was overwhelmed by the almost military precision in which the people who were responsible for building the pyramids worked. The theory that the pyramids were built by people in servitude has recently been blown asunder. People built them because they wanted to – they wanted to be part of Egypt's great and enduring history.

They took pride in their workmanship. They admired and revered their pharaohs and wanted to ensure the safe-keeping of their mortal remains.

I will never ever forget my journey to Egypt. It was a dream come true. I learned an awful lot that I had not known before and I know that there is still much, much more to learn.

As I gazed out over the Great Pyramid from the roof terrace of my hotel, I thought back over the month that I had spent in Egypt and recalled the warmth of the people, especially Mohammed, our tireless driver. I recalled with a smile the laughter when we had danced in the streets during one of the interminable city traffic jams.

As darkness began to fall over the desert, I heard the first call to prayer from the mosque nearby. This was quickly taken up by another and another until the whole air was filled with voices. As I turned to go back to the hotel lounge to join the rest of the crew for a last dinner in Egypt, I saluted the pharaohs and told them that one day I would be back.